Ferguson

Miracle

Steve Stranghoener

This book is dedicated to the Crusaders of Lutheran High School North, St. Louis, Missouri.

"For as the body is one, and hath many members, and all the members of that one body, being many, is one body: so also is Christ. For by one Spirit are we all baptized into one body, whether we be Jews or Gentiles, whether we be bond or free; and have been all made to drink into one Spirit. For the body is not one member, but many." (1Corinthians 12:12-14)

"Then Peter opened his mouth, and said, of a truth I perceive that God is no respecter of persons: But in every nation he that fears him, and worketh righteousness, is accepted with him." (Acts 10:34-35)

INDEX

PREFACE

PART ONE: 2013

PART TWO: 2014

EPILOGUE

2015 – The Legacy Continues

APPENDIX

What is a Miracle?

PREFACE

At this point, I do not believe we need more political or social commentary on the events that exploded in Ferguson, Missouri during the summer of 2014 and echoed around the globe. This book is intended to serve a different purpose. It is the story of life at a small, private school as seen through the eyes of a football coach. Unabashedly and happily sports themed, this saga transcends football. It is a testimony to Lutheran North's impact on the transformation of precious but ordinary lives: students and athletes through their teachers, coaches, administrators and parents.

This is the account of a miracle but it won't be found in gridiron glory or even the shattering events that rocked Ferguson and the world. Accordingly, the title may seem out of place at first, especially since the narrative spans 3 years, well beyond the most intense months of 2014 that launched Ferguson into the international limelight. However, what has been deemed the Ferguson-effect is essential to our tale. Without the stark contrast to the violence, mayhem and chaos of nearby Ferguson, the miracle that is Lutheran North could have been completely overlooked. God can and does use even our worst tragedies to serve His good purposes for us. Such was the case at Lutheran High

School North where peace, joy, patience, understanding and true fellowship prevailed in the midst of the surrounding bedlam.

Miracles occur when God intervenes in the lives of people by contravening natural law as we know it, including the worst aspects of our human nature. I have included a theological treatise on the subject in an appendix if you would like to dig deeper.

For now, there's something we will need on this journey if we want to truly and fully grasp the Ferguson Miracle. We won't be able to recognize it with our eyes alone, not even if we are blessed with 20/20 vision. We'll need to be fitted with special glasses: spiritual lenses.

PART ONE - 2013

Chapter 1: The Lord Works in Mysterious Ways

Who am I to write about the cataclysmic events in Ferguson that echoed around the globe? I'm just a 'privileged' white dude who, at my age, is now fairly well off. While I only live about 10 miles from that community, some might say I'm light years away from the type of struggles and turmoil experienced by the good folks of Ferguson. How could I ever relate to their culture, history and the gut-wrenching emotions seared into their psyches?

I might not be best qualified to offer further commentary on the political, social, or economic ramifications of what occurred in the wake of the shooting of Michael Brown by Officer Darren Wilson. But that is not my purpose. I'm here to offer a different perspective, an insider's eye-witness account of something that escaped the TV cameras. This book is meant to shed some light on a miracle that sprang forth in, of all places, the dusty football practice fields, hallways and classrooms of a small private school only 2 miles from the epicenter of all the mayhem that occurred. For me, this led to an unmistakable conclusion ... God truly works all things together for good (Romans 8:28).

So what was my connection to Ferguson? My immediate ties were quite simple. As an assistant football coach at Lutheran High School North, I had a ringside seat to the events that unfolded in Ferguson in the summer and fall of 2014. However, as I pondered this question in earnest, I realized that my roots ran much deeper there and with a longevity that stretched all the way back to my childhood growing up in the late 50s and early 60s...

This revelation came through a literal trip down memory lane that covered 60 years of history in less than an hour by car. It exposed my personal filters to full transparency, an important element in understanding our story. Despite all the changes that came to Ferguson over the years and the unfortunate circumstances that prevailed recently, I remained favorably disposed to offering an objective viewpoint. This extended beyond Ferguson to some of its inseparable, contiguous communities.

It took me less than 15 minutes to jump on Interstate 270 and head north and east from St. Charles Rock Road in Bridgeton. In no time I arrived at the Florissant Road exit. I could tell I was headed in the right direction because of a billboard advertising the Ferguson Farmer's Market. Hmmm, that didn't sound much like 'the hood' as Ferguson had been depicted on TV. Immediately, I was drawn into the past and my deep connections to Ferguson. Just on the other side of the highway, in nearby Old Towne Florissant, was the first house that my wife and I purchased at 2 Plaza Duchesne. A small 3-bedroom ranch, the master bedroom was actually an addition built above the basement-level garage. Poor insulation made the bedroom floor feel like frozen tundra in the winter. Humble as it was, this tiny, old house served as a big step up from the apartment complexes we inhabited for the first 9 years of married life.

As soon as I turned right onto Florissant Road, another unmistakable blast from the past appeared. My first place of employment after graduating from college was McCluer High School in the Ferguson-Florissant School District. I turned down a full scholarship and departmental fellowship from Washington University that ended my dream of becoming a history professor. One of my college professors offered me good counsel and suggested that I teach high school history to fully gauge my interest before committing another 4 years to graduate school. It provided a wonderful experience. I not only loved teaching history but served as an assistant JV football and varsity track coach.

In football, our Comet JV team was supposed to be fair to middling. Nevertheless, our team played well above expectations. I liked to think, in part, that my youthful exuberance helped. In any case, we put ourselves in a position to play for the conference championship going into our last game against perennial powerhouse Hazelwood Central, also undefeated and heavily favored. This meant a lot to me because I played for the Hawks in high school along with Reid Huffman, the opposing coach.

To give the boys an extra spark, I wore my 1973 Hawk letterman's jacket to the pregame pep talk. I administered a shock treatment by inextricably extoling the virtues of Hawk football, like a lunatic, until the kids were bound and determined to prove me wrong. Well, they shut out the Hawks in a hard-hitting, defensive battle and we claimed the crown.

Ah, those were the days. I really enjoyed the camaraderie we shared. It was a good mix of kids from all over Ferguson and Florissant, with many blacks and whites and a few Hispanics forming a tight-knit band of brothers. Alas, it was not meant to be a long-term endeavor. Harsh reality set in. In 1978 I earned a whopping total of $10,000 a year including my $1,000 pay for coaching 2 sports which, I joked, came to about 25 cents an hour. It clinched it for me when I didn't initially receive a contract for the next year despite admirable performance reviews. I was low man on the seniority pole in a shrinking district. At first, it thrilled me when they finally offered me a contract renewal that summer. Then my bubble burst when I learned that my good fortune resulted from the death of kindly Mrs. Jane Sapp who mentored me throughout my first year.

With my mind largely made up, I gave it another go at Hazelwood West High School where I moved for a little more pay and better job security. It seemed weird to inhabit a teacher's lounge along with people that instructed me in high school. My department chairman was my high school sociology teacher, Mr. Kemper. I enjoyed my brief time there, once I got past the *Welcome Back Kotter* routine, but couldn't escape the economic reality.

Thus, I left my chosen field and went to work at McDonnell Douglas, Boeing today, as a Purchasing Planner C. I thought, *this is why I went to college?* In the common vernacular, my position at MDC sat lower than whale dung at the bottom of the ocean. An erstwhile PhD candidate without a business degree, I served as a glorified file clerk. Ironically though, I received a 40 percent pay increase. Although strangled in the cradle, my brief teaching and coaching career provided valuable lessons that came in handy some 34 years later at Lutheran North.

As I headed south on Florissant Road toward Ferguson, plenty of friendly reminders like January-Wabash Park grabbed my attention. Then, straight ahead, I neared the heart of downtown Ferguson. I knew because I crossed under the railroad trestle. A row of small buildings stood on the right. One once housed the Selective Service Board. That's where I registered for the draft. Luckily, the Vietnam War ended just as I came of age. I felt fortunate back then. Today, I can only think about the sacrifices made by all the veterans who served there. Could I have handled things with such courage and valor considering how unpopular the war was back then?

A few blocks further, I came across the Ferguson Brewery. This brought me to the present for a moment. It heartened me to see a new, contemporary business thriving here. In the blink of an eye, I was transported back to the late 70s and early 80s. Right next to the Ferguson Brewery stood Marley's. In our day, the Golden Greek, as it was called, held special significance since it sponsored our Brighton Apartments touch football team. We had a heck of a team and were, for a good while, the scourge of the Budweiser Apartment League. That group included some of my best friends.

One in particular, Jim Crane, came to mind. That's because he was a Lutheran North alumnus. Back then, no one guessed that he would enjoy unbelievable success as a businessman. Today, among his many other accomplishments, he is the principal owner of the Houston Astros and a great benefactor to Lutheran North.

I spied Suburban Avenue. I needed to turn right and head to Thomas. I lived on this street in Ferguson as a toddler. We weren't there long so my memories were sketchy. Back then, we lived like gypsies. My parents were renters and moved around a lot until we finally settled down in an unincorporated area in the northeast part of St. Louis County. I considered our final stop as my childhood home even though we didn't move there until the fourth grade. In kindergarten, we lived on Aspen Drive in Florissant. I attended Walker Elementary School briefly. Then we picked up stakes for another rental house by Lindbergh and Halls Ferry. I spent second grade at Twillman Elementary School in Spanish Lake. For third grade we moved way over to Duke Drive near Bellefontaine Neighbors and I attended Meadows Elementary School in the Riverview Gardens School District.

Our final destination at 2239 Redman Road was a cracker box house. I didn't care. My dad, a baker by trade, and my mother, an office clerk, worked very hard to afford that house. To me, it seemed like a palace even though we had to panel off a bedroom in the basement to accommodate my big brother, Ray. It was good to finally put down some roots and attend the same grade school, Black Jack Elementary, for more than a year.

I considered our humble beginnings as a blessing. We didn't have a lot of money but possessed everything we needed. Most importantly, my parents brought me into Christ's kingdom through baptism, gave me a Christian upbringing and taught me the value of hard work, dedication and determination. Our modest beginnings helped me relate to some of the good folks of Ferguson and similarly situated students at Lutheran North.

With our nomadic lifestyle in my early years, I couldn't remember a great deal about our time on Thomas Avenue in Ferguson. However, one life-changing event stood out. God intervened through His holy angels when I was 2. As I played off to the side in the back yard one day, my father busily mowed the lawn. The mower struck a nail in the grass and it rocketed across the yard and embedded itself in my chest. It punctured my lung and, according to the doctor, lodged a mere whisker away from my heart. I still bear the mark where the nail entered my chest and a large scar where the surgeon nearly cut my little body in half to dislodge the missile. I thanked God, in retrospect, for preserving my life and believed He had work in store for me, including my time some 57 years later at nearby Lutheran North during the unrest in Ferguson.

This section of Florissant Road by Brotherton Lane is near where my Uncle Irvin and Aunt Dorothy once lived. Some of my McCluer track athletes also resided here when I first coached back in the late 70s. Some things, like the joy of working with high school kids, haven't changed. Take Lee "The Cat" Brown, for example. One of our sprinters, I tried to motivate him with the incentive of a cheap Panama hat. I fashioned it into a collector's treasure with a big, blue, McCluer "M" I painted on the front. I told him I'd let him have it, if he qualified for state. He fell in love with that garish hat, flashed a mile-wide smile and declared, "Coach, yo tempt'n me now!" It only cost me 2 bucks at the dime store but worked like a charm.

The next intersection at Evans Avenue was once home to E. J. Korvette's. Back in the mid-60s it rested on the cutting edge of retail. One of the first stand-alone discount department stores, it supplanted five-and-dime shops like Ben Franklin's and paved the way for today's behemoths like Target, Kmart and Walmart. Only a block away from Interstate 70, I decided to back track for another look having traversed Ferguson from north to south along the western edge. I welcomed the new construction such as Berkeley McCluer South High School. I took a fresh look at residential neighborhoods along the way. These areas appeared a bit run down in places but, for the most part, still represented good places to raise a family.

I turned right and headed to West Florissant Avenue. This route along the eastern edge offered another perspective and included Dellwood and Jennings along with their neighbor, Ferguson. Just a bit further on the left was Royal Furniture, formerly Lammert's. My mom loved to shop for Early American furniture there, especially the Ethan Allen brand.

The former site of one of the best hole-in-the-wall restaurants sat nearby. Arcobasso's, a family run place, featured charming, outdated décor that benefitted from the dark atmosphere. We frequented Arcobasso's for the fantastic food and friendly, homey and casual ambiance. They served their beer in cans. Ironically, years later, the Arcobassos became our neighbors in the Autumn Lakes neighborhood of Maryland Heights. In another quirk of fate, Autumn Lakes was built on the old 9-hole Parkwood Golf Course where their clubhouse,

the Hexagon Hut, served as a watering hole for
Budweiser touch football teams like Brighton.

In the 70s, Peaches Records resided just past the
intersection of West Florissant and Chambers. We
spent a lot of time and money there. In the days
before 8-tracks, cassettes, CDs and MP3s, it was the
place to be. As big as a grocery store, record albums
of every kind and category filled every inch of floor
space. We often spent an hour or more there as we
perused the latest releases and listened to the current
chart toppers that rocked from their radical sound
system. This reminded me how Ferguson once
thrived and offered hope for the future.

An old strip mall that once housed Big Daddy's
Hot Spot rattled my memory banks. I vividly
recalled the night my parents hosted a party at our
house on Redman for my mom's colleagues from
the Printer's Union offices in Pine Lawn. On a
Friday night during my senior year football season,
I observed a strict team curfew. My mom's boss
imbibed too much and Mom didn't think he should
drive home. Thus, Dad rousted me around midnight
so I could help. I couldn't see what happened in my
dad's car but, apparently, the old dude insisted upon
stopping at his favorite bar, Big Daddy's Hot Spot.
My Hazelwood letterman's jacket protecting me
from the brisk fall air, I followed my dad into the
bar to help corral Mom's boss. Inside the smoky

den of iniquity, the Hazelwood High School football coaching staff confronted me. I suffered shock, embarrassment and guilt as I tried to explain my presence to the coaches. A long time passed before I lived that one down. Later I wondered, *what were they doing there?*

I passed Highmont Drive which led to Forestwood Park. Our Brighton football team played a few games there. The scenery changed as I approached Canfield Drive where the shooting of Michael Brown occurred. Once known for its vibrant commerce, blight dominated the landscape. Here, vacant and boarded up buildings offered testimony to the unrest and violence that rocked Ferguson for months. It saddened me to see the aftermath's stark contrast to what had once been. Ferguson's emotional scars were reflected in broken glass, plywood and charred edifices.

Quickly my spirits were lifted by the site formerly occupied by Northland Shopping Center. A magnificent place, it held many cherished memories for me. As a child, I caught the Redbird Express at Northland and rode the bus down to Busch Stadium for Cardinals' Sunday double headers and cheered my favorite player, Lou Brock. As a teen, I saved my money until I could afford to shop for clothes at Boyd's or Famous Barr. When we were first married, Bonnie and I often attended the movies at the Northland Cinema. For some reason, I recalled seeing the original *Longest Yard* there starring Burt Reynolds. I delighted that this spot represented more than a graveyard for dusty memories. Rebuilt, it resembled a beehive of commerce as busy shoppers combed through many fine retail establishments.

On the other side of the street, I noticed the entrance to Emerson Electric. Years ago, when I worked for Anheuser-Busch, I visited these offices to collaborate with some of our procurement peers. We considered ourselves competitors as buyers. Our boss, August Busch III, and Emerson's chief, Charles Knight fanned the flames of the rivalry. The two served on several boards together, including each other's, and occasionally threw down the gauntlet and bragged about how their procurement arms were the best in the industry at containing costs. This often set off a spate of feverish, oftentimes unnecessary activity for whichever side was considered to be low man on the totem pole. Over time, we learned to keep in touch on industry best practices to keep our collective fat out of the fire with the two iconic St. Louis chieftains.

The sight of Emerson's headquarters restored my faith in the community. My company, Anheuser-Busch, fell prey to globalism when we were acquired by Brazilian/Belgian brewer, InBev,

in 2008 for a then-record sum of $52 billion. Other
St. Louis icons suffered similar fates due to the
international mergers and acquisitions craze.
However, Emerson, one of the largest employers in
St. Louis, remained a local powerhouse along with a
few others like Monsanto. What a blessing this
provided to our local economy! Emerson's
continued success, as they plied their trade from
their headquarters near the heart of the Ferguson
unrest, provided a hopeful sign of better times
ahead.

I passed the edge of Ferguson but, instead of
back-tracking, continued on to Lucas & Hunt Road
and turned right. I encountered the tree lined
entrance to Norwood Hills Country Club. I doubted
that anyone who watched the never-ending TV
coverage of the turmoil in Ferguson pictured this as
a location for a staid, old country club. The nearby
residential areas no longer sported the kind of
affluence associated with the country club set. Yet,
there it stood with its fashionable, stately facilities
and two fabulous 18-hole golf courses. Although
never a member of a country club, I knew this place
well.

One of the vendor representatives who called on
me at A-B, Keith Wortman, was a former football
player for the University of Nebraska and the St.
Louis Football Cardinals. He'd never forgive me if I

failed to mention that he won back-to-back national championships as a Cornhusker in 1970 and 1971. As a former Big Red player, he became involved in charitable activities through the NFL Alumni Association. This included an annual charity golf tournament at Norwood Hills. Appropriately, some of the proceeds from the work of Keith and his NFL Alumni pals went to the restoration of some of the St. Louis Public High League football fields. These areas faced challenges even tougher than Ferguson in some ways.

I was privileged to be invited to join Keith in his foursome on a number of occasions. It was quite a treat to meet a lot of football greats who joined in the cause. Like a kid in a candy shop, I relished the chance to rub elbows with the likes of Dan Dierdorf, Jackie Smith, Conrad Dobler, Otis Anderson, Coach Jim Hanifan, Coach Don Coryell and other Big Red stars from yesteryear. It delighted me in particular to make the acquaintance of Mizzou Tiger stars like Mel Gray, Johnny Roland and Roger Wehrli. I loved hearing Keith cut up with Coach Hanifan who was one of the nicest people you could ever meet. He regaled us with stories that made us laugh until we cried. A mediocre golfer on my best day, we never won the tournament, not even close. Yet, I don't think I ever enjoyed myself more. Thanks to A-B, I had the chance to carve a few divots in some of the finest golf courses in the country but none held better memories for me than good old Norwood right near the flashpoint of the Ferguson unrest.

Norwood sparked another fond remembrance for me. While a pariah among St. Louis communities in the eyes of some, ironically, this could not be said of one of our most revered citizens. One year, I arrived late for the sign-up and lunch that preceded the tournament. Keith and the rest of our foursome had already left for the practice range. Since I was starving, I decided to scarf down a burger by myself in the courtyard outside the dining room. Another lonely soul sat at a table on the deserted patio. In a rush, I hurriedly asked if I could join him. He motioned for me to sit down. As I prepared to eat, I finally recognized the kindly, old fellow. To my amazement, it was none other than Stan "the Man" Musial. The sight of him rendered me speechless.

Once I found my tongue, something compelled me to gush about memories from my childhood. It mattered little that he likely heard these kinds of recollections a million times before. To his credit, the living legend seemed genuinely interested as I recounted my first baseball game. In 1963 at the age of 8, my Uncle Leo and Aunt Opal took me and my brother to Sportsman's Park on Grand Avenue,

today the site of the Herbert Hoover Boy's Club.
Although in his last year before retiring, Number 6
smacked one completely out of the park that night.
We beat the hated Cubbies 8-0. Hoarse from
cheering so loudly, I couldn't utter a word after the
game.

With incredible grace and humility, Stan "the
Man" listened patiently as I wrapped up my story.
Mr. Musial, surely the most beloved, iconic figure
in St. Louis, shared his time generously and later
capped the day off perfectly when he regaled us
with *Take Me Out to the Ball Game* on his
harmonica. As I passed by Norwood, my memories
of Stan "the Man" lifted my spirits. Ferguson
suffered terribly but surely could be healed by the
kind of dignity and kindness Mr. Musial embodied.

This road trip brought me full circle,
figuratively and literally. My brief sojourn
reaffirmed that I had much more than a passing
acquaintance with Ferguson. It exposed my old,
deep roots. My fondness for Ferguson and the
surrounding communities proved genuine and time-
tested. My personal time capsule left a distinctly
different impression from the one portrayed on TV.
Ferguson had long been and still was a vibrant
community filled with many wonderful, generous
and friendly people.

Ferguson couldn't be torn apart from the other distinct but interwoven patches in our St. Louis quilt: downtown, the Central West End, Dogtown, Soulard, the Italian Hill, St. Charles, Florissant, Dellwood, Clayton, Kirkwood, Webster, University City, Chesterfield, Ladue, North St. Louis or the Southside. With any fabric removed, including Ferguson, the whole tapestry unraveled.

Chapter 2: Baptism by Fire

With my trek down memory lane finished, there stood Lutheran High School North, home of the Crusaders, on the right hand side of Lucas & Hunt at the crest of the hill. This was where I witnessed the Ferguson Miracle in 2014.

How did I wind up there, of all places, in 2013? I wasn't closely connected to LN other than through friends who attended there. My wife, Bonnie, attended LN her freshman year before transferring to Hazelwood High School where we met. After spending most of my life with other endeavors, my involvement with Lutheran North came down to a twist of fate in the person of Coach Brian Simmons.

In my 20s, after I switched from teaching and coaching, I launched a business career at McDonnell Douglas Corporation and decided to go back to school at night. I earned a master's degree in business management from Maryville University and, after 7 years at MDC, moved to Anheuser-Busch in 1986. As a lifelong St. Louisan, working for A-B represented my dream come true. Good fortune smiled upon me with seemingly endless opportunities to learn and grow. The rewards far outweighed the requisite sacrifices of long hours and the stressful rigors of life at A-B. It accrued to my great privilege and honor to work with such a team of highly gifted and dedicated colleagues. At the top, no one demanded more from his people than the 'Chief', Mr. August A. Busch III. But he also treated us like kings and queens. August III often struck fear in the hearts of many but, by his sheer force of will and incredible talent, commanded our utmost respect and admiration. Fortunately, I enjoyed the bulk of my business career there during some of the best years of St. Louis' finest company, Anheuser-Busch.

The golden age ended with the well-documented takeover by InBev in 2008. I stayed on for a year and a half under the new management but things changed dramatically. By the grace of God, I left under my own terms. It pained employees like me to lose A-B to a foreign investor but at least we benefitted financially. The Brazilians paid a handsome price for the equity that we built up over the years and everyone who invested in A-B stock profited. Able to retire from my business career earlier than anticipated, it gave me the chance to pursue a second career as a writer of Christian fiction from January 2010 through mid-2013.

Although it didn't bring much in terms of financial gains, writing rewarded me in many other ways. It required a lot of time and self-imposed discipline but I loved it. However, after cranking out several books, I needed a bit of a respite. One Sunday afternoon while Bonnie and I visited her parents, I perused their weekly church bulletin from Salem Lutheran in Black Jack and noticed a call for substitute teachers at Lutheran North. I thought, *maybe that's the ticket.* I still had my lifetime Missouri teaching certificate and a passion for history. Part-time work would leave time for my writing and might provide a healthy and meaningful diversion for a while. I thought about going back into teaching full-time when I left A-B but couldn't see myself fitting in at any of the public school districts with my old school beliefs in discipline, personal accountability and the three Rs. My greatest concern was public education's aversion to God and the open expression of the Christian faith. Thus, Lutheran North seemed like a more suitable environment for me.

In June 2013, I was interviewed for a position as a substitute teacher by Mr. Dan Wenger, the Assistant Principal and Dean of Students at Lutheran North. Initially, I felt concerned that even the church and Lutheran institutions like LN were no longer immune to the pressures of political correctness and secularism. Over the course of our time together, Dan allayed any fears I harbored. As represented by him, Lutheran North seemed steeped in the truth and fully committed to propagating the gospel of Jesus Christ. By the end of our session, I felt ready to sign on the dotted line and looked forward to whatever opportunities awaited me as a substitute teacher. Then he surprised me. I didn't know at the time that Dan was an aficionado who played and coached multiple sports including football. In fact, he excelled as a wrestler and earned all-state honors in New York as a high schooler before wrestling some in college too. He caught me off guard and asked if I wanted to tour the athletic fields and I consented happily.

A stylish fence separated the school grounds and athletic fields and, as we approached the gate, I noticed a bronze placard emblazoned with the image of my old pal Jim Crane. It read, James R. Crane Athletic Complex. This brought flashbacks of our misspent youth with the bad boys of Brighton. A dusty buzz of activity caught my eye with summer football practice underway. This took me back to my years at Hazelwood High School. This conjured a few less than idyllic memories as I recalled 2-a-day practices in the upper 90 degree heat. Back in the day, our coaches prohibited ice at practice and even frowned upon water as being only for sissies. Instead, we received as many salt tablets as we could keep down. We complained at our own peril. No one wanted to incur the wrath of D-line Coach Tom Dubis with his Popeye forearms, cement-block body, tree trunk legs and massive head topped with a shock of unruly orange hair. We aptly labelled him the Great Pumpkin ... but, wisely, only behind his back.

A figure approached from the midst of the football frenzy and snapped my wandering mind back to attention. Were my eyes playing tricks on me? No, it was my old friend, Coach Brian Simmons. He caught me off guard because, the last I knew, Coach Simmons recently took over as the head coach at football powerhouse Hazelwood East. To my delight, there he stood as the new head football coach at Lutheran North. We chatted and reminisced for a while and then he dropped the bomb on me. He advised me of an open position and asked if I'd like to be an assistant coach on his staff. I almost laughed it off since it had been 34years since I coached high school football. Yet, something intrigued me, so I heard him out.

I had a great deal of respect for Coach Simmons. Beyond his impressive record of accomplishments as a football coach at places like Pattonville, Hazelwood Central, Cardinal Ritter and Hazelwood East, Brian served as an assistant under iconic coach Don Greco when my son, Eric, played football for Pattonville. Although Eric became a record setting quarterback on the only Pattonville football team ever to play for the state championship in the Dome in 2000, he wasn't much more than a question mark when he started out as a freshman. As Coach Simmons liked to say, "Eric was a kid that came in at 5'5 and 120 pounds soaking wet and it took a full minute for him to run a 40-yard dash." The hyperbole aside, it was, in essence, the truth. Somehow, Coach Simmons possessed the keen eye and wisdom to recognize the heart and fire inside of Eric and helped him develop into a baller. What he lacked in size and pure athletic ability, he made up for with hard work, determination, smarts and reckless abandon as a cornerback under Coach Simmons' tutelage. Somehow that year, the skinny kid won the top freshman honor, the Willie Robinson Award, despite Pattonville's bevy of talented freshmen. Thereafter, Coach Greco was instrumental in Eric's development as a quarterback.

Coach Simmons possessed a unique talent. Eric often told me how Coach would pull a 'Simmons.' That's the term Eric used to describe Brian's uncanny ability to read offenses and defenses and predict how plays would unfold before they happened. Eric's favorite story was when Coach Simmons talked to him between plays during a game and told him exactly where to stand. He

predicted that, if Eric followed his instructions to a
T, he'd get an interception and a chance to run it
back for a pick 6. Eric listened and, amazingly, it
transpired just as Coach Simmons said it would. I
had many chances to personally witness Coach's
special gift from the sidelines at Lutheran North.

I tried to back out. I hemmed and hawed and
pointed out how time had passed me by. I had good
reasons to turn down Coach's generous and
flattering offer but he was patient, persistent and
persuasive. Coach wasn't pushy about it. His
subtlety snuck up on me. When I pointed out that I
couldn't contribute much from an Xs and Os
standpoint, it didn't faze him. He said they had
plenty of Xs and Os guys. Somehow he convinced
me that I could add something abstract to the mix. I
had no intention of coaching high school football; it
was the last thing on my mind. But my admiration
for Coach Simmons proved to be the clincher. I had
come to serve as a substitute teacher and somehow,
inexplicably, left as an assistant football coach.

A good month passed before I overcame my
hesitancy and gave into Coach Simmons' magic
spell but, once I acquiesced, I felt excited about my
new pastime. Football has always been a passion of
mine. As a youngster, I never played Pop Warner
football, Khoury League baseball or any kind of
organized sports for kids. My hard working parents

didn't have time for such luxuries. So I got together
with the neighborhood kids on the sandlots and we
did it on our own. My lack of experience didn't stop
me from making the football team at Hazelwood
High School. However, after I graduated, I knew I
didn't possess the skills to play in college at a place
like Mizzou. But there were intramurals and, after
leaving college for the real world, touch football
leagues around St. Louis. I watched countless
football games, cheered on the Missouri Tigers
from little past infancy and followed the Big Red
and later the Rams religiously. I never lost interest
in high school ball and regularly attended
Hazelwood Hawk games and switched allegiances
to the Pattonville Pirates when my kids attended
school there.

Shedding the ties that bound me to Hazelwood
seemed almost impossible. When our oldest child,
Steve, started attending Pattonville High School in
the mid-90s, I rooted for the Pirates every chance I
got, especially when it came to Steve's hockey and
volleyball games. Football was another matter.
Once, I got busted by Steve and his classmate, Chris
Eggert, when they caught me sneaking over to the
visitor's sideline as Pattonville faced the Hawks at
home in the playoffs. They ribbed me mercilessly
and I slung it right back at them, Hawk style. I liked
to remind them how we manhandled the Pirates

back in the day. This remained a major point of contention until one day when I produced my Torch Yearbook and showed them how we pasted the Pirates 54-13 my senior year.

As for Lutheran North, regretfully, I once looked down my nose a bit at the Crusaders. Where I came from, the Suburban North Conference reigned. To me it represented the Big 12 of high school football in St. Louis and everyone else took a back seat, especially the smaller schools like LN. We never played teams from the Metro Conference like LN, John Burroughs or Country Day since they were smaller and several class sizes beneath us. My bias favored the bigger schools and I focused my attention mainly on the winning legacies of outfits like the Hazelwoods, McCluers, Riverview and Pattonville.

I wasn't completely unaware of the rich football tradition of Lutheran North but, I guess, chose to ignore it. Looking back, I was pretty foolish. The Crusaders captured 5 state championships in football and put numerous players into the NFL. In the 70s Mark Petersen played for the KC Chiefs and his brother Kurt, a Mizzou grad, played for the Cowboys. They grew up less than a half-mile from my house on Redman Road. The 80s yielded a bumper crop of Crusaders. Bobby Edmonds played for the Seahawks and Buccaneers, Thomas Rooks with the Vikings and Cardinals, Tony Buford with the Big Red too, Clarence Woods with the Saints, Linzy Collins, another Mizzou grad, with the Packers and Steve Atwater with the Broncos and Jets. Atwater, known as the 'Smiling Assassin', was one of the hardest hitters in NFL history, named All-Pro 8 times and won 2 Super Bowls. More recently, Robert Douglas of the Class of 2000 played with the New York Giants.

The fact that my buddy, Jim Crane, went to Lutheran North didn't sway me at first. He didn't play football there anyway. He starred in basketball and baseball. In fact, scouts considered him a pro prospect as a pitcher until he blew out his elbow throwing for the Mules of Central Missouri State. Although his baseball career was cut short by an injury that, today, could have been overcome by Tommy John surgery, he did alright. If you can't beat 'em, join 'em and if you can't join 'em, then buy 'em. He purchased the Houston Astros and turned the hapless losers into a playoff contender. Everything Crane-o touched turned to gold. Not one to forget his humble roots, Jim Crane blessed many people through his hard work, business acumen and charity. His beneficiaries extended far and wide but his generosity toward his alma mater helped alter my view of Lutheran North.

Recounting some of LN's rich history, including
Jim Crane's era, provided a revelation similar to the
one I apprehended cruising through Ferguson. Gary
Mantei, a mutual friend through Jim Crane, also
became a successful businessman and generous
benefactor to North. Moreover, he still followed LN
football since he once roamed the gridiron as a
Crusader. However, my ties with him extended
beyond our ties to Jim Crane. I remembered
competing against him in softball in the LC-MS
Church League years before. This made me think of
my good pals, Steve Burroughs and Dennis Lueck.
They both graduated from Lutheran North with Jim
Crane and were good athletes in their own right.

I met Steve and Dennis through our
congregation as fellow members of Trinity Lutheran
Church in Bridgeton. We all played softball
together when we were young enough to compete
for championships. Dennis was a clutch hitter in
addition to being our pitcher. In warm-ups he
always dazzled me with his softball knuckleball.
His son Andy, whom I referred to as Superstar,
flashed some amazing leather for Trinity at
shortstop during our comeback year. With me and
several others in our late 50s, a core of young guys
consisting of Andy and my sons, Steve and Eric,
convinced us to give it one more shot. We barely
had 10 guys, just enough to field a team. We did so

with the addition of our former slugger, Herbie Harrington, and his contemporary, Ken Nissing, both even older than me. In storybook fashion, we won the league championship before we hung up our cleats for good. My ties to my LN pals remained strong even after Steve Burroughs moved to Detroit.

The more I thought about it, the closer I felt to Lutheran North. For such a relatively small school, familiar Crusaders seemed to pop up all over the place. One of the young, up and coming stars that once worked for me in Procurement at Anheuser-Busch, Andrew Davis, graduated from Lutheran North. I loved debating the merits of Hawk versus Crusader football with him. As much as I denigrated Andrew's alma mater, tongue-in-cheek, I secretly admired LN. Although not in the vaunted Suburban North Conference, they resided up north and ... practiced Lutheranism, like me. With apologies to all my Roman Catholic friends, it warmed my heart every time the undermanned Crusaders beat one of the larger, more privileged Catholic schools in the area.

Only a month until the start of the season, I walked past Crane-o's smiling bronze image as an assistant football coach for the Lutheran North Crusaders. Honestly, had I looked into a crystal ball; I might never have donned a Crusader shirt or cap. I told Coach Simmons I wanted to hang it up within 2 weeks of starting at North. What had I done? I seemed like an old dinosaur with both feet stuck in the La Brea Tar Pits. The past caught up to me with a vengeance and I slammed into 'football present' like it was a brick wall.

The world changed dramatically since the time I played and coached high school football. The shotgun and pistol formations didn't exist then. The QB always lined up under center. The offense consisted of a few basic formations. Usually, the running backs were split behind the quarterback in a pro-set. One or maybe 2 wide receivers lined up along with perhaps a tight end. Consequently, defenses were also pretty bland. Shifting or substitutions occurred infrequently. We ran into something unusual like a wishbone attack occasionally or some other variation of the option. Sumner High School stood out because of its wide open running attack with multiple backs, shifts and counters but they were an exception. Back then, even much of college and professional football featured rudimentary approaches compared to today.

At Hazelwood, we considered our offense exotic because we regularly shifted between a pro set and power-I where the fullback lined up directly behind the QB in a 3-point stance, with the flanker back directly behind the fullback in a 2-point stance. We had a superstar named Pete Blake as our flanker back. A Parade All-American who received offers from all of the major, Division 1 universities, he chose to accept a full ride to Mizzou. Because of Pete's exceptional talent, our coaching staff redesigned our entire offense to feature him as a running back and receiver. From the power-I we ran him off tackle, swept around end or ran an option with quarterback Dan Allison. Pete also posed a dangerous threat on screen plays out of the backfield. Oftentimes we'd shift Pete from the power-I to the slot and involved him in the passing attack as a receiver. He led the team in receiving and rushing. We had never seen anything close to him before 1972 when, with Pete leading the way, we averaged better than 30 points a game and claimed Hazelwood's first state crown. Technically we were co-champs due to a horrendously muddy field that left the final game in a tie.

What I experienced as a high school player, coach and fan seemed like child's play compared to what I encountered at Lutheran North. Even the most Plain Jane offenses we faced were much more sophisticated than anything we encountered back in the 70s. With Lutheran North on the cutting edge, my anxiety soared. The offense included 15 different formations and we used them all. The QB lined up under center, in the pistol or all the way back in the shot gun. Our basic offense consisted of a spread with 4 receivers and a single running back. Sometimes we'd empty the backfield and go with 5 receivers. Depending on the formation, our receivers might line up as a pair of twins or a single on one side and triplets on the other. Often, the inside receivers lined up in the slot or in tighter as wing backs just outside of the tackles. Tight ends entered into the mix as well. They shifted all over the place with the wings, slots or wide receivers coming in motion on the jet to fake a handoff or run the ball.

My confusion mounted since we didn't have a playbook to study. The coaches wanted the players to keep things in their heads. To make matters worse, I missed out on more than a month of practices. The early sessions offered the chance to get to know the players' names and positions and become familiar with the offensive and defensive schemes under less pressure. Since I missed those practices and trailed everyone else by 30 years, I felt significantly disadvantaged. At least I was allowed to work with the receivers and defensive backs which helped a little since I had been a receiver. Even that didn't provide much of an advantage. In my prime, one could learn what we referred to as a route tree fairly easily. Less complicated then, the guy on the left might run a deep fly and the receiver on the right might run a post or a slant. At North, with so many formations and 4 or 5 receivers on any given play, the task proved much more difficult.

The amount of time required to coach football caught me off guard. Foolishly, I thought I could write in the morning and spend part of the afternoons at practice. My first encounter with HUDL convinced me that I might never catch on. Although still unclear, I assumed the acronym reflected the home turf of the founders; a bunch of self-described tech-nerd jocks out of the Haymarket District in Lincoln, Nebraska. Maybe the letter "u" was added to make it relevant to football and capitalize on a clever play on the word huddle. When I played in high school, we were lucky to get a single film of one of our opponents. We may have spent, at most, a half-hour reviewing film each week but usually we only went to such lengths for big games and the playoffs. HUDL took this to a whole new level, light years ahead of anything I knew

HUDL reflected our high tech, digital world. With it, we logged onto a site on a PC or smartphone and gained immediate access to video from every game, every opponent and not just the current season but years past too. It also allowed us to review all of our own games from the present and past.

We even recorded and rehashed our practices. I reviewed video on HUDL for 2 to 3 hours daily before practice. Additionally, I spent time playing catch-up in learning our own offenses and defenses and all of the newfangled terminology. Putting names with faces added to the task. This included the coaches too. With 8 others besides me, it took a while to keep Brian, Jon, Kelvin, Josh, Mike, Mike, Matt and Troy straight. This was supposed to be a fun diversion for me but my head almost exploded. Coaching wasn't the temporary, casual respite from the rigors of writing I envisioned.

This was a full-time job! In the mornings I studied football. Practices stretched through the afternoons into early evening. On game day we got together around 8:30 on Saturday morning and prepared the field or loaded up the buses for a road trip. We watched film, reviewed the game plan and assignments, got the kids taped up and took the field just before noon for warm-ups. The games lasted until 4:00 or so and then we helped clean up the field and broke down the game until 5:00 or later. I missed watching Mizzou football on Saturdays. I learned firsthand the dedication required to be a high school football coach. It was full-time, 7 days a week and the season extended well beyond

August through October. Practices started shortly after the school year ended and, with any luck, the season stretched into late November with a good playoff run. Important duties carried over into the off season: new player orientation, player development, training for coaches, clinics, banquets and more.

Much time passed before I processed my dilemma into something positive and constructive. It ultimately left me with great admiration for the dedication and skill of Brian Simmons, Jon Mueller, Kelvin Austin, Josh Cody, Mike Lorenz, Mike Williams, Matt Hieke and Troy Fehrs. It also dispelled stale stereotypes about football players being a bunch of dumb jocks. These lessons escaped me at first when I was lost in the maelstrom. I felt like a man with his hair on fire. Operating in full panic-mode, I had no time to ponder the virtues of the coaching profession. I quickly concluded that I was horribly misplaced.

Coaching obliterated my normal routine. I wanted a counter-balance to provide a break from writing, but it seemed an either/or situation. Coaching didn't leave enough time to pursue my craft in earnest, even part-time. I missed normal dinnertime with Bonnie, meetings with our regular Monday evening dinner crew and fraternizing with family and friends on Friday evenings. Weekends were totally discombobulated; not only Mizzou football but Saturday morning adventures with the grandkids were out of the question. Although difficult, disrupting daily rituals was not the biggest stumbling block I faced.

The beating my ego took bothered me the most. Despite my best efforts, I didn't seem to catch on very well and found myself far behind the curve. This made it difficult to contribute much to the team. I felt like a liability rather than an asset. It appeared that time had passed me by. I struggled as an old guy in a younger man's world. The other coaches played in college and many had years of contemporary experience under their belts. Compared to them, I felt more qualified to be a water boy than a coach. I soon realized there was a big difference between an arm chair quarterback and actually knowing something about the game. I excelled in the business world as a successful leader. It pained me to find myself trailing the pack in football. What was supposed to be a fun, frivolous diversion instead made me feel miserable.

When I told Coach Simmons I was ready to hang it up, he listened patiently in his typical fashion. Then, he politely tried to change my mind, without pressuring me. He reiterated that he had plenty of Xs and Os guys. Coach said I could contribute in other ways. He laid out the intangibles such as building character and offering motivation. In my pessimistic state of mind, this didn't help much. However, Coach Simmons didn't give up easily. He implored me to give it time and assured me it would all begin to click for me soon. When my reluctance didn't wane, he threw in the kicker … "think about the kids." *Yeah, do it for the kids*, I thought. He also lured me with the promise that it would be a lot more fun once we started playing games. His magic worked and I decided to stick it out for a while.

As promised, I became more acclimated in the weeks that followed, with the help of Jon Mueller and Troy Fehrs. Jon was a young guy by my standards; 30 years my junior. Nevertheless, I considered him an offensive guru. He served as North's Offensive Coordinator in addition to his duties as Athletic Director. Jon put together a makeshift playbook for me with various diagrams and provided rosters and other information that I could study on my own. Troy allowed me to horn in on his territory working with the receivers and defensive backs during individual drills. That's where I felt most comfortable. He also did something much more important in making me feel like part of the team. Troy taught theology at North and, thus, coordinated and usually led team devotions and prayers. He gave me a regular slot in the weekly rotation so I could take advantage of an area of strength.

I felt like I finally contributed in a small way and became more familiar with the scheme of things by using Jon, Troy, Coach Simmons and the others as sounding boards. Just as my outlook took a more positive turn, the end of August 2013 came. Finally, the time arrived to play some real football instead of grinding it out in practice week after week.

First up, we faced the Clayton Greyhounds on Saturday, August 31st. It thrilled everyone as we finally went through our Saturday morning game day preparation and headed out before the fans at Lamothe Football Field. Clayton represented a nonconference foe and, like most of our opponents, a bigger school. Lutheran North resided in Class 2 with Clayton in Class 4. The same size disadvantage held true in the Metro Conference where John Burroughs and MICDS occupied Class 3 with Westminster in Class 4. This didn't bother us, though. Going in, many considered Lutheran North as a probable favorite over Clayton. This proved to be a horrible assumption.

In the extreme heat of that day, we wilted like a bunch of morning flowers. As we approached the half, our players appeared fatigued and cramped up constantly. As Coach Simmons put it, one might have thought a sniper lurked in the press box since so many Crusaders sprawled on the ground and winced in pain. The game turned ugly. We fell behind early and then, frankly, gave up as the Greyhounds manhandled us. The anticipation of a grand opening to a championship season blew up in our faces.

The disheartening loss seemed inexplicable since we featured a plethora of huge lineman. Our offensive line averaged over 280 pounds per man. Our skill positions overflowed with talented players. Our quarterback, Justin Baker, already a seasoned veteran as a junior, established several records the year before. Our new head coach, a proven winner, left one of the state's elite programs at Hazelwood East to guide us to victory. Yet, our visions of glory were snuffed out on day one. Clayton trounced us 34-7 and we looked pitiful in the process. Talk about depressing! After 2 months of hard practices, what did we have to show for ourselves?

Thankfully, we didn't have to wait long for a chance at football redemption. We collectively tried to shake it off and get on with our pursuit of a championship. Next up, we traveled to Priory, an affluent, private Catholic School. Although a week into September, the seemingly endless summer still dogged our trail like a hungry bloodhound. By 1:00, the temperature soared above 90 degrees again. Like the week before, we didn't hold up well under the heat. We started out okay but succumbed to the pressure when we fell behind the Rebels. Perhaps our inability to handle adversity revealed a character flaw. Regardless, we took another beating and lost 33-14 to a team that, by all accounts, we might have vanquished on a good day. It felt like a trend rather than an aberration.

We worked hard to exorcise our football demons but somehow couldn't shake the uneasy feeling that permeated our practices. Maybe we needed some home cooking but, for the second week in a row, we traveled on the road, this time to Westminster Christian Academy on September 14th. WCA's impressive campus and football stadium loomed large. Their stately buildings and state-of-the-art football stadium dripped money. They didn't contend with natural turf like us but, instead, boasted a pristine, high-tech, artificial surface. The heat persisted and lingered like an obese monkey we couldn't get off our backs. Stuck in a rut, we experienced similarly depressing results against the Wildcats. Westminster bludgeoned us 31-14. At 0-3, panic threatened to set in. Even the coaches had a hard time staying motivated as we watched our dreams die on the turf.

Fate toyed with us cruelly and we searched for a break. We needed to push around a lessor opponent to boost our dwindling confidence. Unfortunately, we returned home and faced perennial powerhouse, John Burroughs. In 2012, they graduated running back Ezekiel Elliot who moved on to Ohio State and became a Heisman Trophy candidate. We hoped they hadn't reloaded with another stellar back. Wrong! John Moten stood ready to fill Elliot's big cleats. He ran through us like green stuff through a goose. Our vaunted Crusader offense finally got untracked and put up 35 points on the Bombers. However, they still trounced us, 69-35 and had quite a time as they celebrated in front of us on Lamothe Field.

We hit rock bottom at 0-4 and I felt miserable. I didn't sign up for this. What did we have to show for our hard work but pain and disappointment? I dejectedly thought … *I had it right in the first place. Why didn't I stick to my guns when I resigned weeks before?* This presented a real quandary. I could have pulled up stakes before without much consequence. In my mind, it would have amounted to addition by subtraction. Before, the team seemed destined for greatness with or without me. Calling it quits now would be cowardly. I couldn't stoop to being a quitter … no way. Plus, I thought about the kids. In the preceding 2 months, I became acquainted with many of the players and a bond formed. It seemed rotten to leave them in their time of dire need.

I decided to stay and ride it out. Like everyone else, I felt awful. We knew football required everyone to fight through adversity and take the good with the bad. But none of us anticipated such an unmitigated disaster. Big losers at 0-4, our prospects going forward appeared bleak. The forlorn look on Coach Simmons' face hurt the most. As a fighter, he never backed down from adversity but he proved human like the rest of us. It wasn't the string of losses that ate away at him but rather the fact we seemed unable to get through to the kids.

We had plenty of size, speed, talent and experience. We possessed all of the elements necessary for a championship, except for one thing. The Crusaders lacked heart. Apparently, the guys didn't have the will to win. Our frustration mounted during our baptism by fire and I wanted to escape but couldn't pull the rip cord under these circumstances. I felt compelled to stay for Coach Simmons, the other coaches and the kids ... and myself. No matter what happened, I needed to stick it out. I resigned myself to the notion that the pain couldn't last much longer. At the rate we were going, an early end to the season seemed probable.

Chapter 3: Off the Radar

Football kept me as busy as a one-legged punter, so I didn't have a lot of time to ponder deep thoughts. Politics and sociology experiments had no place in high school sports. At first, I didn't take much notice of the positive atmosphere at predominantly black Lutheran North. Race relations never seemed to enter into the equation on the football field or anywhere else on campus. The coaching staff, spilt about evenly between black and white, remained completely united from the outset. Maybe that's because misery loved company and we had plenty of football angst to go around. When I looked at Coach Simmons, I didn't see a black guy and when he looked at me, I wasn't a white dude. We were friends, plain and simple. As coaches, we saw each other as brothers. Maybe we were brothers from another mother but brothers nonetheless.

You can tell when racial issues are simply being well-managed. Things are calm and cordial to the naked eye. A cross word is never spoken. Tact and diplomacy aren't necessary because anything even potentially controversial is kept bottled up deep inside. Racial consciousness may permeate the air but there's never an outward sign. Emotions are held hostage by political correctness. Thoughts that have even the slightest potential of offending anyone are beaten back by hyper-alert consciences. There might be a bubbling cauldron somewhere under the surface but one would never know it from the calm exterior.

This was not the case at Lutheran North. The camaraderie, brotherhood, sisterhood and true fellowship weren't manufactured. We didn't have to walk on egg shells. That's because we didn't practice race relations but engaged in human relations, based first and foremost on the love of Jesus Christ. It made for a wonderful, edifying and peaceful experience ... even if we were 0-4.

In this idyllic setting, we seemingly operated in a vacuum, far from the troubles besetting the world around us. Perhaps our lack of awareness wasn't a bad thing in that it allowed everyone to focus on academics, sports and preparations for life after high school. But, in time, it became impossible to ignore things that were not on our radar screen then.

Tensions mounted in our country but these pressures remained nearly imperceptible to us. Volatile substances that existed outside our protective cocoon seeped in but through tight filters and seemed inert and harmless to us. We were vaguely aware of something that had made the national news years before in 2009 but it had little tangible impact on the environment at LN. The media labelled it the Beer Summit. It became the first time, as far as I recalled, that an ostensibly local news story took on national prominence due to the President's personal involvement. It set off a chain of events that continued to echo thunderously across our nation and defined a new, unfortunate era of race relations in America.

There were varied accounts but, in brief, the story went something like this. On July 16, 2009, Sergeant James Crowley of the Cambridge Police Department arrested Henry Louis Gates, a Harvard professor and acquaintance of President Barack Obama, for disorderly conduct. Professor Gates returned to his rented Cambridge home after an overseas trip and had trouble with the lock on the front door and entered through the back way. Someone called the Cambridge Police and reported a possible break-in. When Sergeant Crowley arrived on the scene, he found Professor Gates still trying to work the front door open from the inside. Sergeant Crowley tried to establish Professor Gates' ownership and asked for his identification. The officer claimed that Professor Gates wouldn't cooperate and started hurling angry charges of bias and racial profiling. Purportedly, Sergeant Crowley issued multiple warnings before he arrested the recalcitrant professor.

An objective observer could see aspects of both points of view. Who wouldn't be angry for being confronted by the police for allegedly breaking into his own home? We might all be short tempered after a long, tiring trip followed by a stubborn door lock. On the other hand, wouldn't most of us be thankful to know the police were looking out for our interests in our absence? Nevertheless, it's easy to see how a highly respected, black professor from one of the nation's most prestigious, Ivy League universities might feel cynical toward a white police officer rousting him in his own home. What cop wants to take grief from a citizen and be labelled a racist just for doing his job? Perhaps, given time, this would have blown over and cooler heads would have prevailed without the incident turning into an ugly, divisive national debate. We will never know. When the President of the United States became involved, the national spotlight inevitably followed.

Politics entered a new era with our first black Commander-in-Chief. It was fairly early in President Obama's first term and the media wasn't about to let the opportunity to explore race relations pass. Perhaps the President should have deferred until all the facts were available and the local justice system's process had fully played out. Maybe he shouldn't have commented publicly on a local police matter at all. Then again, he occupied the ticklish position of knowing the Professor personally and, fairly or unfairly, shouldered the expectation of being the standard bearer for minorities everywhere. Some might have complained that he was the President of all Americans and not just the minorities. Whatever the case, he said this when questioned by the media. "I don't know, not having been there and not seeing all the facts, what role race played in that. But I think it's fair to say, number one, any of us would be pretty angry; number two, that the Cambridge police acted stupidly in arresting somebody when there was already proof that they were in their own home, and, number three, what I think we know separate and apart from this incident is that there's a long history in this country of African Americans and Latinos being stopped by law enforcement disproportionately."

Whether one agreed or disagreed with the comment, one thing was sure. The President didn't mince words or sit on the fence. He came down squarely on the side of Professor Gates and summarily indicted law enforcement officials everywhere. His comment that the police acted stupidly really infuriated law enforcement and seemed, to many, an uninformed rush to judgment.

Others hailed him for finally standing up for the oppressed minorities. The President touched a chord that lit a firestorm of opinions.

In an effort to quell the dissension and restore calm, the President walked back his earlier comments during a press conference on July 24, 2009. He said, "I want to make clear that in my choice of words I think I unfortunately gave an impression that I was maligning the Cambridge Police Department or Sergeant Crowley specifically — and I could have calibrated those words differently." He also stated that, "I continue to believe, based on what I have heard, that there was an overreaction in pulling Professor Gates out of his home to the station. I also continue to believe, based on what I heard, that Professor Gates probably overreacted as well."

This helped but didn't really resolve things. The racial animus horse couldn't be led back into the barn. The President went further and tried to create what he termed a "teachable moment" on race relations. Mr. Obama called both parties together for a Beer Summit at the White House on July 30, 2009. He and Vice President Joe Biden sat together with Professor Gates and Sergeant Crowley in the Rose Garden. It was great political theater and all parties presented a peaceful, even cordial picture for the press. Comments made afterward were not so reassuring. No one apologized. Sergeant Crowley maintained that he followed proper procedures in making the arrest and Professor Gates declared they still had their differences. Although the President made a good, conciliatory effort, he didn't admit any error in getting involved and never retracted his, some would say, jaded and incendiary view of race relations.

The President succeeded in one regard. He got the incident off the front pages. On the surface, this left us with nothing more than silly, light-hearted ponderings of the press. Everyone wanted to know what kind of beer they drank. As it turned out, President Obama had a Bud Light, the VP sipped a Buckler, Professor Gates downed a Sam Adams and Sergeant Crowley enjoyed a Blue Moon. On this issue, I stood firmly in President Obama's camp. As an Anheuser-Busch guy, it pleased me to see that the President selected our best-selling brand. While the Beer Summit smoothed things over, the issue remained far from dead. The Beer Summit left an open wound that continued to fester even if it largely escaped our limited purview at Lutheran North.

The next incident that stirred this pot of unappetizing stew occurred during the off season so; it affected us coaches only minimally. However, no one at Lutheran North escaped the media storm that followed. A 'white man', George Zimmerman, shot and killed a 17-year-old, black, high school student named Trayvon Martin in Sanford, Florida. Zimmerman was actually of Hispanic/mixed-race origins but, the press initially characterized the shooting as a white-on-black killing. The media seized on the opportunity to promote a narrative claiming a serious racial problem in the United States. At that time, it seemed unclear whether a connection existed between the two high-profile incidents. Nevertheless, the nation's mood shifted. Anger and resentment surfaced and the media quickly fanned the flames.

News coverage depicted Trayvon as an angelic victim, cut down by a ruthless vigilante fueled by racial animus. The pictures of Trayvon circulated in the media made him look like an innocent waif. I may have been more prone than some to withhold judgment and wait for all of the facts to play out. Perhaps my age, experience or natural skepticism toward the media helped. Still, the coverage played on my emotions too. Naturally, people jumped to conclusions in pondering the tragedy. Did Zimmerman really have to shoot him? He was only a kid! Then gut reactions changed as more of the story unfolded. Trayvon's pristine past crumbled. For one thing, the truth didn't fit the image of a 98-

pound weakling. Zimmerman insisted that Trayvon Martin attacked him and pounded his head into the sidewalk. Zimmerman felt Trayvon threatened his life and forced him to use his weapon in self-defense. The release of some photographs showing a bloody, swollen nose and lacerations on the back of his head supported Zimmerman's claims.

This cast things in a different light. As usual, it appeared there were two sides to the story. Wouldn't it be best to let the justice system sort things out rather than prosecuting the volatile situation in the court of public opinion? Unfortunately, cooler heads didn't prevail before President Obama jumped into the fray again. This elevated things to a fever pitch. Intentionally or not, the President served notice to the country and the world that the time had come to tackle, once and for all, the ugly truth about race relations in America. As with the Beer Summit, the President reacted swiftly and decisively. He didn't parse words or opt for some type of middle-of-the-road, conciliatory compromise. The President chose sides and reacted before he had all the facts. President Obama left no doubt regarding his feelings when he made this statement during a press conference on March 23, 2012, "If I had a son he would look like Trayvon."

So; was Trayvon Martin the victim of a gun-toting, vigilante bigot? Or did he, a street-tough, drugged-up thug in a hoodie, beat the living daylights out of hapless George Zimmerman who had no choice but to defend himself? A vast gulf existed between these polarized views. Everyone had an opinion it seemed, from everyday citizens, media-types, celebrities and activists like Al Sharpton, all the way up to the President of the United States. The Beer Summit may have placed an unlit fuse near a powder keg but this was altogether different. The Trayvon Martin incident set the timer on a 'nuclear bomb.' Intense, non-stop coverage roiled the controversy. However, the lid on our national pressure cooker remained intact while the wheels of justice ground slowly.

It was no easy task for the justice system to sort out the facts in this case. The investigation dragged on for 6 weeks under heavy scrutiny and pressure until murder charges were issued against George Zimmerman. It took over a year for the attorneys to prepare their cases. Consequently, our "national tragedy", as President Obama deemed it, sat on the back burner until the trial finally commenced on June 10, 2013. This brought the topic of race relations back to the fore.

At Lutheran North, we proceeded with business as usual for the most part. The students enjoyed the summer break from classes while the football players prepared for the next season. By the time I joined the staff in mid-summer, we commenced with applying the finishing touches to the 2013 edition of Crusader football. And the trial of George Zimmerman came to a resounding conclusion. The jury acquitted Zimmerman on July 13, 2013.

Shortly thereafter, President Obama seemed to reveal his personal investment in the case when he stated the following at a press conference, "Trayvon Martin could have been me 35 years ago." Did the President feel a miscarriage of justice occurred? It appeared that way to some. To others he simply displayed his emotions and remorse over the loss of one so young. Whatever motivated him, one thing was clear. The matter of race relations in the United States remained unsettled.

We didn't toss political footballs at Lutheran North but limited ourselves to the genuine leather kind. You could say the same for the academic halls. Current events broached the classrooms but the media or politicians didn't hold sway over the prevailing mood. Being in an atmosphere where Christian principles abounded really made a difference. Nevertheless, everyone was exposed to the news of the day and we all led our separate lives away from the school.

The matter of Trayvon Martin surfaced at North rather innocuously for me. One day I noticed one of those brightly colored rubber bracelets used to promote popular causes. It appeared on the wrist of our running backs coach, Kelvin Austin. Out of curiosity, I asked him about it and he showed me that it contained 2 words, "Trayvon Martin".

I immediately regretted my casual inquiry. Obviously, Coach Austin had adopted the cause which, I assumed, revealed his stance on the matter. I struggled to respond. If I disagreed in any way or took exception, would it lead to a dispute? Would it fracture the budding bond that we shared as members of Coach Simmons' staff? The chances seemed good. How could a white guy and black dude cross swords over such a controversial subject without it becoming a racial thing? Surely we couldn't tread on such dangerous ground without something unfortunate happening. Yet, nothing of the sort took place. That's because Kelvin and I and the other coaches practiced human relations.

Did I share any common ground with Kelvin? At the time, he was 32 years my junior at only 26 years old. Barely older than my baby girl, Chelsea, it seemed we didn't even speak the same language at times. He often sang the lyrics from rap tunes completely foreign to me. I only recited words penned by Lennon & McCartney or some other old fogies. At best, I ripped off a few Run DMC stanzas that must have seemed ancient to him. How could

an old, white geezer relate to a hip, young brother?
The old adage that opposites attracted proved
accurate because I gravitated toward Kelvin almost
immediately. Like me, Kelvin Austin was a
Hazelwood Hawk. Once a Hawk, always a Hawk. It
didn't matter that I graduated in 1973, 14 years
before he was born. We shared common ground,
solid ground. We weren't a black kid and a white
old guy. Kelvin and I both had black & gold
running through our veins.

Something else drew me to Coach Austin. I
enjoyed his youthful enthusiasm. It took a few years
off my life. He infected those around him with his
joyful exuberance for the game. He took his craft
seriously but carried on in jaunty, lighthearted
manner that kept things fresh and fun. I relished our
little side conversations and the insights they
provided. For example, one of the oddities I
unearthed was that Kelvin considered himself
somewhat of a wresting aficionado. This provided
for some more common ground since I too got a
kick out of the outrageousness of the old-time
grapplers. Our histories overlapped with the likes of
'Nature Boy' Ric Flair, Ricky Steamboat and
Jimmy 'Super Fly' Snuka. Sure wrestling of this
sort was fake and silly but it provided us with a lot
of laughs.

The most important thing I learned about Coach
Austin was his Christian faith. Although not a
Lutheran, it didn't matter in terms of our friendship.
Of course, I couldn't read his heart but his faith was
manifested in his works. Our righteousness, the
justification of Jesus Christ, is outside of us. We're
not Christians because of our good works. Good
works don't precede faith but rather flow from faith.
James, under God's inspiration, said as much in
verse 2:20 of his epistle, "But wilt thou know, O
vain man, that faith without works is dead?" Some
have erroneously interpreted this to mean that we
must perform good works to apprehend faith. Good
works are the result of having the free gift of God-
given faith. Christians can't help but try to do the
will of God. Here's how it is stated in Matthew
7:17, "Even so every good tree brings forth good
fruit; but a corrupt tree brings forth evil fruit." The
tree produces the fruit and not vice versa. God
makes good trees, not us.

Kelvin was a good tree. Did I ascertain this from
his charitable endeavors? No. Kelvin manifested his
good fruit through his love of Jesus, the Incarnate
Word. It also showed in his love of God's word as
revealed in Holy Scripture. Kelvin seemed to
gravitate toward me too. For some reason, when we
got on the subject of current events or other general
topics of the day, Coach Austin seemed eager to

hear my biblical take on things. He possessed a genuine thirst for the truth of God's word. Our conversations sometimes took a spiritual turn that edified him and me. I found it easy to admire his faith and reverence for Scripture.

This Godly attitude seemed prevalent amongst all the coaches. Others besides Kelvin and I broached the subject of Trayvon Martin. In a few conversations, several of us chimed in together. We checked our emotions at the door and a calm approach prevailed at North. Another young black man, Coach Josh Cody, thirsted for the living water of the Incarnate Word. When a group of us first dissected the Trayvon Martin case, two separate narratives surfaced as influenced heavily by the media. While I had been exposed to what I considered both sides of the story, some of my peers apparently had not.

This could have put us at odds and caused knee-jerk reactions and heated conflicts. Instead, people listened and weighed things before getting entrenched in a particular position. It reminded me of the Christians in Berea mentioned in Acts 17:11, "These were more noble than those in Thessalonica, in that they received the word with all readiness of mind, and searched the scriptures daily, whether those things were so." It didn't say the Christians in Berea immediately accepted what Paul said at face value. They listened though and went back to see if his teachings were consistent with Holy Scripture. They didn't lean solely on their own understanding but used the word of God as their guide and the final arbiter of the truth.

What could have been an uncomfortable situation when the topic of Trayvon Martin came up proved to be nothing of the sort. In a relatively short time, Kelvin and I hit it off along with the other coaches. A level of mutual respect came from getting to know each other as people rather than as black and white or young and old. We engaged in human relations, not race relations. Would this have happened in another setting outside of Lutheran North? Possibly, but I doubted it. Our common, earthly purpose as Crusader football coaches bound us tightly together. More importantly, we shared a spiritual bond as brothers in Christ that the peaceful confines of Lutheran North helped to nurture.

We didn't have to stick our heads in the ground like ostriches and avoid any mention of Trayvon Martin in order to sidestep the controversy swirling around the subject. The bonds of peace we shared in Jesus Christ helped us to approach things differently than we likely would have otherwise. A certain patience and willingness to listen existed. It didn't mean we shared the exact same view, but it helped us elude the trap of painting each other into a corner by stubbornly adopting intractable, polarized positions. The Godly atmosphere at North helped us to keep our priorities in order. That is, God's will came first and everything else followed thereafter. Helping the kids took priority: athletically, academically, socially and spiritually.

Chapter 4: Fellowship

How we, as coaches, got past the thorny issue of
Trayvon Martin and George Zimmerman without
being ensnarled in the type of controversy
experienced by so many others spoke volumes, not
only about Crusader football but Lutheran North in
general. Let's face it though; the faculty, students,
coaches, athletes, parents and administrators at
Lutheran North were no different than people
anywhere else when it came to our old, sinful
natures. We were all desperately wicked (Jeremiah
17:9), corrupted by sin from conception (Psalm
51:5) and dead in our trespasses and sins apart from
Christ (Ephesians 2:1). As bad trees we couldn't
produce anything but bad fruit. However, through
baptism or a later conversion by the power of the
Holy Spirit working through the word, we were
born again from above and given new natures, in
Christ, to go along with our 'Old Adams' (2
Corinthians 5:17).

As Christians, we were no longer slaves to sin.
Apart from Christ, we could only sin and rebel
against God. Our new natures allowed us to seek to
know and do God's will. And the Holy Spirit
sanctified us toward holy living. We received this

power every time we dined on the life-giving, spiritual food provided in the Holy Bible (John 8:31-32).

Did this mean that Christians, including the folks at Lutheran North, were home free to sin no more? Of course not since nothing was further from the truth. We knew this by observing our own behavior and listening to our consciences. We still sinned grievously every day, all day long, in thought, word and deed. This didn't come as a surprise. Declared righteous by God in Christ, we still awaited to be made righteous by shedding our sin-corrupted flesh, either in temporal death or by the miraculous conversions of our bodies, in the twinkling of an eye, on the final day of judgment at Christ Jesus' return (1 Corinthians 15:52).

Atheists, secular-humanists, agnostics and Bible-scoffers of every stripe loved to label Christians as hypocrites because of our sins. We recognized that being Christians didn't make us perfect. To the contrary, as miserable sinners, we desperately needed the Savior and His forgiveness. Our guilt and shame could only be covered by the blood of Christ that made us saints in spite of our sins. This notion seemed foolish, in an earthly sense, but reflected God's truth. Even when we transgressed against our God, we remained saints in

His eyes because of the miraculous, cleansing power of the blood of Jesus Christ (Isaiah 1:18).

This dichotomous condition applied to ALL Christians, even those considered the best among us. All of the great heroes of the Bible sinned grievously. Some of God's most faithful, noteworthy servants committed some of the worst transgressions recorded in Scripture. Take Moses, for example. He murdered an Egyptian. In cowardice, Abraham tried to pass his wife off as his sister to avoid King Abimelech's wrath. Years later, Isaac, the child of promise, pulled the same despicable stunt as his dear, old dad with his own wife Rebekah because of his fear of the Philistine King.

Do we have enough time to cover all the sins of conniving Jacob who gave rise to the Twelve Tribes of Israel? And what about the dastardly deed perpetrated by 11 of his sons who sold their brother, Joseph, into slavery under the Egyptians? Surely the bearer of God's promise from Jacob's line didn't partake of this skullduggery, right? Think again because Judah led his brothers in wanting to murder Joseph before Rueben convinced them otherwise. Then there was the Apostle Peter, the Rock. He denied Jesus 3 times in the Temple courtyard and even cursed vehemently as he spewed his back-stabbing lies.

Some misinformed Christians considered Mary immaculate and without sin. How could this be? God clearly declared in Romans 3:23, "For **ALL** (emphasis added) have sinned, and come short of the glory of God." God offered no exceptions. This included the heretical notion of praying to Mary for salvation. God left no doubt about this in Acts 4:12, "Neither is there salvation in any other: for there is none other name (Jesus) under heaven given among men, whereby we must be saved." Listen to what Mary confessed in Luke 1:46-47, "And Mary said, my soul doth magnify the Lord, and my spirit hath rejoiced in God my Savior." Mary acknowledged her common plight with all of us sinners. Accordingly, her joy overflowed in proclaiming her salvation from sin through our Savior, Jesus.

Has anyone ever gone as far as the Apostle Paul in propagating the gospel of Christ in spite of all manner of pain, toil and peril? Well documented in the Bible, he committed many terrible acts before his conversion on the road to Damascus. He persecuted the church and orchestrated the murder of many Christians.

What happened after his glorious conversion? Paul remained a sinner. He said so himself. In fact, he called himself "chief of sinners" (1 Timothy 1:15). He didn't exaggerate but meant it sincerely. This applied as much to us as it did Paul. How

could we be Christians since we sinned so
grievously and so often even though we, like Paul,
knew better? Was that how we showed our
appreciation to Jesus?

Thankfully, Paul, under God's inspiration, gave
us the answers in Romans 7 & 8. He lamented
sincerely, like we often did in repentance when
confronted by our sinfulness, that he did things he
knew were wrong and didn't do the things he knew
he should. It reflected the essence of our old
natures. He went on to explain how the 'Old Adam'
in us was still present and battled constantly with
our new natures. That's what made us sinners and
saints at the same time. The old nature remained a
slave to sin whereas the new nature looked outside
to Jesus Christ for power and guidance.

In the end, we, like Paul, could cast off
melancholy and joyfully declare as he did in
Romans 7:24-25 and 8:1-2, "O wretched man that I
am! Who shall deliver me from the body of this
death? I thank God through Jesus Christ our Lord.
So then with the mind I myself serve the law of
God; but with the flesh the law of sin. There is
therefore now no condemnation to them which are
in Christ Jesus, who walk not after the flesh, but
after the Spirit. For the law of the Spirit of life in
Christ Jesus hath made me free from the law of sin
and death." Still sinners, Christ freed us from

condemnation by taking the punishment we deserved.

What set things apart at Lutheran North if not the people, admittedly a bunch of miserable sinners? The answer could be summed up in one word: fellowship. A lot of people considered fellowship as sharing good times together. To some, this came when gathering around a box of donuts with some fresh, hot coffee. For others, it occurred while cheering on a favorite sports team. Still others thought fellowship meant enjoying a favorite movie together.

Fellowship is more than togetherness or a mere social gathering. True fellowship is marked by shared beliefs ... not just any beliefs but the most important ones pertaining to life, both temporal and eternal. Here's how God puts it in Ephesians 4:4-6, "There is one body, and one Spirit, even as ye are called in one hope of your calling; One Lord, one faith, one baptism, One God and Father of all, who is above all, and through all, and in you all."

True fellowship is shared by those who believe in the same God and not just any God but the One, True and Triune God. This is God the Father, Son (Jesus Christ) and Holy Spirit. It also refers to shared beliefs in time and eternity based on the truth of God's word; not our own understanding or flawed human reasoning but the revelation of God in His word. True fellowship also involves common practices, like baptism and the Lord's Supper, that are carried out in accordance with God's will as expressed in His word.

A common bond, call it school spirit, exists at all schools, public and private. Perhaps it is expressed in the school colors, fight song and alma mater. There can be a sincere sense of loyalty and togetherness. But this is different than true fellowship. True fellowship is shared by Christians who are called to faith by the power of God's Holy Spirit working through the word. It is an eternal bond that is nourished, maintained and strengthened by God's word.

This bond set us apart at Lutheran North. Perhaps not everyone in and associated with Lutheran North shared true fellowship. Only God knew for sure. This type of fellowship wasn't exclusive to Lutheran North. The bond of true Christian fellowship extended across the globe. An invisible, eternal bond, it included believers everywhere. It formed a great, cosmic plethora of branches that stretched worldwide with each one attached to the same vine: Jesus Christ.

Nothing special existed in the brick and mortar that formed the walls of Lutheran North. The landscaping consisted of ordinary trees, bushes, flowers and grass, all destined to wither and die eventually. The secret wasn't even in the cross that sat atop the spire, a mere symbol of something much greater. The people that occupied its buildings were ordinary human beings; sinners prone to all sorts of bad behavior by nature. Yet, a special bond of true fellowship existed at Lutheran High School North in St. Louis, Missouri.

The people were transformed by the power of the Holy Spirit and grafted into the True Vine. All members of one body, the body of Christ and born again from above, we possessed new natures eager to serve the Lord. This was accomplished apart from us, solely by Jesus Christ. We believed this by God-given faith granted to us by grace. The inspired, inerrant word of God sustained and strengthened us in this bond of fellowship. Yet the question remained. Could it withstand the destructive forces, only a few blocks away, that threatened to tear apart our nation?

Chapter 5: Storm Clouds Gathering

Sometimes we, like Christians of old, expected our lives to be rosy all the time. We gushed with optimism and showed great fervor in sharing the gospel of Christ when things were going our way. However, as the 'Old Adam' in us was wont, we tended to fall apart when storm clouds gathered. Recall how bold Elijah skedaddled when faced with Jezebel's death threat. Peter, the Rock, showed his zeal for the Lord by leaving the boat to walk out on the water to meet Christ. When he took his eyes off the Savior and noted the fierceness of the wind-driven waves, he began to sink. As recorded in Matthew 26:35, Peter boasted vehemently that he would die before he would ever deny Jesus. When push came to shove, we all know how that turned out. It was silly for us to expect a rose garden when Jesus warned us of the very opposite, many times. Take Luke 21:17 for example, "And ye shall be hated of all men for my name's sake." Then there is 2 Timothy 3:12, "Yea, and all that will live godly in Christ Jesus shall suffer persecution."

Life's troubles aren't limited to the persecution of Christian believers. Everyone faces adversity sooner or later. Such difficulties aren't limited to persecution or animosity. We're all too familiar with the bad fortune this world so often serves up. Is there anyone who hasn't been touched by illness, shame, embarrassment, pain, sorrow or countless other adversities? For every blessing there seems to be a curse and the litany is endless. Then there is the big one. The darkest black cloud of all is death. No one can escape it. We shouldn't be surprised by the sad state of the world. God has chronicled how this came about through Adam and Eve's fall into sin. His perfect world was corrupted through and through. This pertains not only to sinful human beings but extends to the entire creation, the whole universe down to its very core elements. God teaches clearly that it's foolish to think we can turn this world into some kind of utopia. There will always be war, famine and poverty. God pointedly warns that He is the only one that can fix this world. He is going to do so by destroying the existing, sin-corrupted heavens and earth and replacing them with new, perfect ones.

In the meantime, where does this leave us? In a fix. We're messed up people in a wretched, decaying, doomed world. This is beyond any doubt for believers and non-believers alike. The only question is how are we going to handle the situation? Some people deny the existence of God and say it's just the way things are, so deal with it.

What a hopeless outlook on life that would be!
Other people want to blame God and hurl insults at
Him. I wouldn't recommend that course of action
any more than I would suggest spitting into the
wind. Lots of people think we can make this world
a better place. This is true in a spiritual sense and
even temporally to a point but we're wasting our
time if we expect to achieve utopia. Tackling
climate change, achieving social justice, or chasing
other contrived crusades won't fix the real problem.
We should all try to improve things as best we can
but only if we keep temporal matters in perspective
within God's eternal plan of salvation.

In some ways, I'm the poster boy for being a
fair-weather Christian. I'm cranky when I get
hungry, impatient with others, a sore loser and I
have a hot temper. It's hard not to get frustrated and
feel like giving up when one takes a look at our
world. It's topsy turvy when it comes to justice. It's
just not fair! Everybody knows it. The harder we
try, the worse things get. It's clear that we're
fighting a losing battle, so why bother? What's the
point? Even in a spiritual sense, things can look
hopeless. Christians always seem to be on the losing
end of things. Kindness is met with disdain,
mockery and loathing. Truth yields only anger.
Turning the other cheek gets you 2 sore cheeks.

We're supposed to walk by faith and not by sight. No matter how bad things may seem, there are better days ahead in a spiritual sense. Our prospects in this world often appear so bleak. Yet, Christ never leaves us to twist in the wind. Listen to this solemn word of encouragement from Jesus in John 16:33, "These things I have spoken unto you, that in me ye might have peace. In the world ye shall have tribulation: but be of good cheer; I have overcome the world." Christ also promises that we're not in this by ourselves. In fact, He declares that He is always with us, (Hebrews 13: 5-6 & 8 and Matthew 28:20) ... "Let your conversation be without covetousness; and be content with such things as ye have: for he hath said, I will never leave thee, nor forsake thee. So that we may boldly say, The Lord is my helper, and I will not fear what man shall do unto me. Jesus Christ the same yesterday, and today, and forever" ... "and, lo, I am with you always, even unto the end of the world. Amen."

Even as a football coach, I knew that the best pep talks never emanated from a locker room. For the greatest source of hope and encouragement, we needed only turn to the Scripture. It never failed, no matter how far we may have slipped into the *Slough of Despond*. All I needed to do was look at Christ's life to make my troubles seem miniscule and complaints petty. He suffered such pain and torment for you and me. He literally sweated blood in the Garden of Gethsemane. Jesus was mocked, beaten, tortured and hung on a cross. He had the power to call down legions of angels in His defense or to crush all of His enemies merely by saying the word. Yet, in humility, He allowed Himself to be punished as the lowest form of criminal even though He was perfect, sinless and holy before His accusers. Jesus took our sins upon Himself, became sin for us (2 Corinthians 5:21) and suffered the wrath of the Father, an eternity of hellfire, that we deserved before giving up His life to save ours eternally.

How could I have been so foolish as to worry about being 0-4 as a football team? Why would I let my personal frustrations, worries and minor inconveniences get the best of me? Hadn't Christ already secured the most important victory for all time and eternity and handed the trophy, a crown of eternal life, to you and me? It was all summed up in that final word He declared loudly from the cross (John 19:30), "Tetelestai" or, in our English, "It is finished" or more accurately from the Greek, "The debt is paid in full!" Our toughest foes ... sin; death and the devil ... have already been vanquished. When our old, evil foe, Satan, came prowling around us we could frighten him away with one, little word: Jesus. Even at the very end of life in this world we could confidently proclaim these words from 1 Corinthians 15:55, "O death, where is thy sting? O grave, where is thy victory?" This we could pronounce with all surety because of the glorious resurrection of Jesus Christ in which we shared.

It's hard to be anything but joyful, even in the midst of adversity, when basking in such love; the underserved, unconditional love of Jesus Christ. Unbelievers can't understand it. To them it seems like foolishness but, as Christians, adopted sons and daughters of Almighty God, we can find true peace in the midst of the worst earthly circumstances possible. Here's how Christ put it in Matthew 5:11-12, "Blessed are ye, when men shall revile you, and persecute you, and shall say all manner of evil against you falsely, for my sake. Rejoice, and be exceeding glad: for great is your reward in heaven: for so persecuted they the prophets which were before you."

As always, I kept my head on straight by sticking my nose in the Bible. It never failed to provide the perfect remedy when an attitude adjustment was needed. God's word helped to put things in perspective. It afforded the long view. Temporal matters were cast in a different light when seen through eternity's prism. Big problems turned into tiny troubles. Impassable, cavernous canyons shrank down to inconsequential cracks and creases in the sidewalk. When Christ spoke of affluent people, those in love with money above all else, having a tougher time getting into heaven than a camel going through the eye of a needle (Matthew 19:24), his disciples lamented because they knew this was true for all of us regardless of wealth. They realized that none of us had the power to put God first due to our sinful human natures. The disciples questioned whether anyone could be saved. Our Lord assured them in verse 26, "But Jesus beheld them, and said unto them, with men this is impossible; but with God all things are possible."

Coach Lombardi once famously said, "When the going gets tough, the tough get going." Those were good words of encouragement for his Green Bay Packers and football players everywhere. In a much higher way, Jesus offered reassurance and inspiration to us all. No matter what we faced and no matter how steep the odds were stacked against us, we could take heart in the words that God revealed through Paul in Romans 8:31, "What shall we then say to these things? If God be for us, who can be against us?" This was true for the young prophet, Jeremiah, when he was gripped with trepidation over the prospect of proclaiming God's word to powerful, unwilling, scornful listeners in Judah. In verse 8 of chapter 1 of his inspired book,

Jeremiah received this assurance from God, "Be not afraid of their faces: for I am with thee to deliver thee, saith the LORD."

The earthly obstacles we faced at North paled in comparison to such serious, spiritual matters. Did our next opponent, the Lutheran South Lancers, represent such a threat? With my mindset properly adjusted and heart in the right place, a football game didn't seem like much to sweat over. Then again, we lost to South the year prior on September 21, 2012 by a score of 62-52. This represented an anomaly for more than the outlandish assault on the scoreboard. Since its founding in 1965, Lutheran North suffered few losses to the Lancers. In fact, no one readily recalled the last victory by South in the rivalry game. Coach Mueller thought it might have been 27 years prior in 1985. The debacle for North in 2012 showed that anything could happen. The possibility certainly existed that we could find ourselves in an even deeper hole at 0-5, if we took South lightly. We needed to get down to business.

Coach Simmons provided the kind of leadership we needed. Although unaccustomed to long losing streaks, Coach handled the situation with aplomb. He never wavered in setting the team's sights on making the playoffs and aiming for a state title regardless of how unrealistic, even ludicrous this might have seemed to others at the time. There was nothing contrived in his unshakable confidence. The coaching staff believed him and, most importantly, so did the players. Coach Simmons served as our anchor in the storm. With his rock solid, calming influence to steady us, we concentrated on the business at hand with a true sense of purpose.

When that Saturday, September 28th, 2013 rolled around we went through our normal game day routine. We gathered in the film room about 8:30. First we studied ourselves and our opponent. At Coach's urging we constantly strived to find ways to improve. Motivational clips got our juices flowing. In finalizing our preparations, we reviewed the offense, defense and special teams' assignments and plans for the day. After taping and dressing out completely, we took the long walk from the locker room down to Lamothe Field. Rather than hooting and hollering, an eerie quietude accompanied us. This didn't reflect fear or apathy. To the contrary, the quiet confidence Coach Simmons instilled in everyone bubbled just below the surface. We didn't need to show our resolve through histrionics. Like silent assassins, we approached the field ready for battle. We were determined to let our actions speak louder than our words.

A high level of competition was required to share a true rivalry. The St. Louis Cardinals and Chicago Cubs have been heated antagonists throughout much of Major League Baseball history. However, much of the sizzle dissipated over the past decade due mainly to the futility of Chicago's North Siders. Cubs vs. Cards games still attracted large crowds and some fanfare but lacked the old passion. That changed in 2015 when the Cubs experienced a much anticipated resurgence. Cards' fans certainly regretted being bounced out of the playoffs by the Cubbies but, all-in-all; it was a good thing in that it restored the rivalry to rightful prominence.

The same thing happened with the North vs. South battle of the Lutherans in 2012. It shocked North but breathed new life into South's moribund program. In 2013, the Lancers came fully prepared to extend their newfound dominance. They must have sensed North's vulnerability at 0-4. The visitor's sideline crackled with energy.

Early on, South appeared to be overmatched. With an apparent edge in talent, we moved the ball at will and lit up the scoreboard. Then the tables turned. As North poured it on, South refused to give in. We punched and they counter-punched. Every time we appeared to pull away, they made a run at us. A comeback victory by our cross-town rival loomed large with a dismal 0-5 record a real possibility. Much of the blame rested with our own mistakes and lapses. But considerable credit went to

South. They brought the fight to us with plenty of heart and spirit.

In our 4 previous games, we suffered under a disturbing trend. When the going got tough, we folded up our tents and went home. Rather than rallying together and fighting through adversity, we consistently wilted under pressure. Despite the wide spread in our 4 losses, we could have won some of those games under the right circumstances but we lacked a fighting spirit. Would we fall prey to apathy and cowardice again? If so, it would sound the death knell for our 2013 aspirations. This time though, a different attitude prevailed. As these storm clouds gathered, we didn't back down from the challenge. We came together that day as one. The Crusaders faced adversity and prevailed 44-33. The final score belied the game's closeness but that didn't change the outcome. More than our first victory, the win represented a reversal of fortune … a resurrection of sorts. Finally, we were a team.

From a football perspective, we witnessed a break in the clouds. A bright beam of warm sunshine streamed through the darkness. Our first win, especially the way we overcame the struggles that had haunted us through the first 4 games, gave us an incredible lift. Looking straight ahead with new confidence, we saw clear, heavenly, azure skies. With our focus so locked in on the business ahead, some other dark clouds escaped our vision. Outside of our peaceful, happy confines at Lutheran North, darkness pervaded. Trouble was ever present in spite of the fact it largely escaped our attention.

Sometimes when you look far out on the horizon and see pillars of clouds forming it's hard to sense the danger. Often, they can pass by without ever bringing a drop of rain. Or they just might carry the destruction and devastation of a howling, rampaging twister. If you've ever lived through a tornado, you know that they can come up almost instantaneously and catch you unawares despite all our fancy meteorological technology.

In our case, the clouds outside of our view represented a still undefined threat. Trayvon Martin's death was no longer in the headlines but it hadn't faded completely. Usually, even the biggest stories faded away as a result of our 24/7 news cycle and the public's insatiable appetite for the next batch of dirty laundry. However, the Trayvon Martin story and, more importantly, the troubling social issues it raised, never went away. Fed by anger, it survived and slowly morphed into growing unrest.

Chapter 6: Band of Brothers

You can get acquainted with people during good times but it's different when you've shared a row boat in stormy seas. We suffered miserably during our 0-4 start but, from hindsight, I realized it was a blessing. I knew my fellow coaches well enough as colleagues and enjoyed working with them. However, I didn't fully appreciate and admire them until we faced adversity together. Our bout with tough times burned away the dross and revealed the precious metal beneath.

Our shared calling transcended football. The Crusaders represented more than a team; we formed a family and saw the players as our own kids. We wanted the best for them in everything. Our care and concern extended well beyond the gridiron. Academics commanded much of our attention. And keeping them out of trouble took preference too. Did they have their priorities in life straight? Could they handle adversity off the football field? Life's problems, dangers, challenges and opportunities loomed. They needed to be more than just athletes. Would they be well-rounded individuals able to support themselves, lead productive lives and have a positive impact on our society and world? Most importantly, we wanted to help sustain, grow and strengthen their faith in our Lord and Savior Jesus Christ unto life everlasting.

I already knew Coach Simmons as a friend and someone I admired and trusted. However, working as part of his staff and seeing how he conducted himself day-to-day in the heat of battle cast him in a different light. It provided me with a new level of respect for him. He really cared about the kids. I suspected that many high school coaches, especially those in public schools, didn't have the time, inclination or opportunity to delve too far into off-field issues, particularly when it came to spiritual matters. Naturally, they wanted to get down to the business of football. As much as anyone, Coach Simmons demanded that the kids know their football. He relentlessly preached learning their assignments, honing their techniques, polishing their skills and understanding our opponents. Yet, he made time for regular lessons on family life, academics, spiritual matters and life in general in the real world.

Coach Simmons started every practice with a team chat. He discussed football sometimes but more often covered events of the day. Coach railed on anyone who brought shame upon themselves and the team by getting into trouble or failing academically. Sometimes he seemed merciless in administering tough love. He wanted to drive home the point that there's more to life than football. Stated plainly, academic and deportment standards took precedence over football. Coach Simmons didn't sugar-coat the fact that most of our players weren't destined to make it to the next level. Thus, classroom work commanded a higher priority in preparing for the life ahead. Coach took personal interest in the lives of his players, both in school and on the home front. It pained us when he laid some of these personal issues bare but he always had the best interests of the kids at heart.

If someone botched things up in school, Coach considered them fair game. Such incidents provided many a teachable moment for all the kids. However, he handled personal family problems differently. Coach Simmons spent many hours dealing with heart-rending problems on the home front. They ranged from marital to financial issues and everything in between. Coach served as a mentor or even a substitute father to those in need. He provided the kind of moral support and service that extended far beyond anything in his job description. The coaches kept the kids' personal matters private to avoid embarrassment. About the only time we discussed family matters openly occurred when someone used mom or dad as an excuse for bad behavior. If a kid blamed his parents for missing practice, Coach lambasted him as "a pampered momma's baby." While fierce, such criticism often proved comical. I think the kids appreciated his no-holds-barred honesty.

Coach Simmons was no ogre. Although normally easy going, nothing solicited a tirade from Coach quicker than when he received complaints about players from teachers or administrators. He refused to tolerate bad behavior, apathy or laziness. Coach Simmons was definitely old school, if you considered instilling the characteristics of accountability and personal responsibility as old fashioned. Sometimes the lessons came in the form of a tongue lashing. Other times there might be sprints, laps or push-ups. I think one of the harshest and most effective punishments he meted out was the opposite of corporal punishment. Once, when a player's behavior in school shamed the entire team, Coach Simmons didn't waste a lot of words or extract a physically demanding pound of flesh. Instead he brought a folding chair to practice and sat it at the base of a steep hill bordering the practice field. He dispassionately outlined the infraction and then advised the perpetrator to sit and relax while all of his innocent teammates ran sprints up the hill, over and over. The young man in question, seeing his innocent teammates punished for his transgressions and with sheer agony on their faces, hurt more than if he'd suffered through a hundred sprints himself. It brought Christ Jesus to mind.

No sadist, Coach Simmons genuinely cared for our players. He knew such drastic measures kept the guys on the straight and narrow path. Sometimes during our pre-practice talks, he literally came to tears in sharing the hard truth about life's dangers. Coach recounted stories of years past at other schools where someone got off track and wound up with a pregnant girlfriend, in jail or even dead. He cautioned, "Don't let a few minutes of pleasure leave you with a lifetime of responsibility." He never pulled his punches when required but didn't dwell solely on the negative. Oftentimes he talked about former players that achieved success through hard work and dedication; sometimes in football but more often in other walks of life. Coach provided positive role models when he invited former players to talk to the kids.

The quality I admired the most about Coach Simmons was the way he allowed for spiritual enrichment. It required vigilant time management to squeeze in the team's work, especially later in the season when the sun went down early. Yet, Coach never scrimped on the time apportioned to sharing the truth of God's word. I'm sure he felt pressured to get on with business but it didn't show. He always gave the Lord His due for the sake of the kids. This impressed and uplifted me. The daily devotions often contained a football analogy but not always. In either case, a strong element of faith existed, apart from football and rooted firmly in the Holy Scriptures.

Coach Troy Fehrs led and organized this wonderful endeavor but many others participated too. Coach Mike Lorenz, a regular participant, always gave a rousing testimony to the joyous truth of the gospel. Coach Jon Mueller's devotions exhibited a deep and abiding faith that belied his youth. Our daily walks through Scripture included others besides the coaches. The thing that delighted me the most about Lutheran North was the way that everyone and everything seemed geared toward a singular purpose. We helped each other grow in truth and faith through the power of God's Holy Spirit working through His word. Our Dean of Students, Dan Wenger, generously and enthusiastically participated in this endeavor. Our Principal, Tim Brackman, took time out of his challenging schedule and prepared thoughtful devotions that he shared with the team. The President of the Lutheran High School Association of St. Louis, Tim Hipenbecker, also shared heartfelt devotions with the kids despite the demands on his time. This provided a great blessing and gave us all a sense of true fellowship, not just as a football team but within the entire community at Lutheran North.

Coach Simmons juggled spiritual demands and football needs adroitly. It required tremendous time in focusing on the latter but he never cheated the kids by limiting the former. As probably the worst offender, I was often verbose when it came to devotions. As one of my passions, I sometimes went to great lengths in sharing the good news. However, even though I undoubtedly tried his patience, Coach Simmons didn't cut me short. Maybe I abused the privilege but, all-in-all, the kids profited. At least that's the impression I got from some of their feedback. It definitely proved to me that Coach Simmons was not just paying lip service to the Lord. His care for the kids, in all aspects including their spiritual lives, proved completely genuine.

I think Coach Simmons' empathy for the kids was borne out of his own past. You might say he graduated from the School of Hard Knocks. As the product of a single family home, he related to some of our players who faced similar challenges. Brian and his two older brothers were raised by their mother, Dorothy Simmons. As a young child, Brian struggled in school. He didn't make excuses but the Public School System in St. Louis did not serve him well. His mother worked hard enough to not only raise her three boys but somehow afforded placing Brian in the Catholic School System in the fifth grade. Thereafter he turned his failures into achievements and graduated from Bishop Dubourg High School with a 3.0 GPA. He went on to Missouri Valley College and continued to excel. Brian maintained a 3.2 GPA while playing football for MO Valley. He graduated in three and a half years and earned a B. S. degree in Business Administration in 1989.

Some guys were good at talking the talk. Coach Simmons walked the walk. Every day he woke up before the crack of dawn and provided study hall supervision to kids with failing grades. He didn't just preach the importance of a good education, he led the way. Coach could have been the casualty of a dysfunctional school system at an early age. Young Brian could have made excuses and played the victim. Perhaps he would have descended into a life of drugs or crime as many others did under similar circumstances. But that didn't suit Dorothy Simmons or her baby boy, Brian. The work ethic he showed by graduating in such fine fashion from Dubourg and Missouri Valley continued on throughout his life, up to and including his time at Lutheran North. Brian Simmons went on to earn several advanced degrees going to school at night, on weekends and online: MBA, Fontbonne, 1995;

MS Athletic Administration, William Woods, 2013 and MS Ed. (Teaching Certificate), Lindenwood, 2015. As of this writing, he was on track to complete his MS Ed. Administration in May 2016. Beyond coaching, teaching and his continuing education, Coach Simmons started up several successful small businesses.

In a life filled with much success and many noteworthy achievements, one setback stood out as the toughest and most regrettable: his divorce. Coaching required an incredible amount of time and this put undue pressure on the marriage. A bitter pill for anyone regardless of the circumstances, Brian and his family suffered devastating consequences that lingered for years. Despite this unfortunate chapter of Coach Simmons' life, he persevered as a faithful father and grandfather.

The success Coach Simmons achieved as an athlete prior to his coaching career wasn't an easy ride either. Although fast and gifted athletically, he lacked a football player's size. Brian started playing organized football at the age of 10 as, of all things, a defensive end. His first team, the Royal Knights, cut him unceremoniously. From there, he moved on to the Mathews-Dickey Boys Club where he hoped to play tailback. It never materialized since Mathews-Dickey had a plethora of good running backs. Brian wound up playing center. It provided little consolation at the time but Brian's coach assured him that learning the center position and toiling as a lineman would make him a better running back in high school. His JFL coach was either prophetic or perhaps just a good salesman.

When he finally made it to high school at Bishop Dubourg, he surprised his coaches with his athleticism. Brian quickly proved to be a special player, one with a small body but big heart. The undersized, misplaced JFL lineman finally got his wish and moved to skill positions on offense and defense as a running back and defensive back. As a freshman, Brian played a few games on the JV team but quickly moved up to the varsity. From there, as they say, the rest was history. Brian Simmons piled up school records and many accolades thereafter, making all-conference teams and then all-district and state. Nothing changed at the next level. He made second team all-conference as a freshman running back at Missouri Valley. He repeated this feat as a senior. Brian Simmons even earned a tryout with the Kansas City Chiefs in 1989. Although he didn't make it into the NFL, the little kid initially cut by the Royal Knights left an indelible mark. He earned membership in the Bishop Dubourg Hall of Fame and Missouri Valley College Hall of Fame.

After his playing days ended, Coach Simmons didn't rest on his laurels by reliving the glory days. He preferred the here and now and the future. He committed his life to helping others fulfill their dreams using football as a springboard to higher and more meaningful things. That's how I took the measure of the man. I also judged the content of his character by looking at the people around him. Coach Simmons exhibited stellar judgment in choosing his staff.

I was the odd duck on Coach Simmons' staff. Everyone else played college ball. When I graduated from Hazelwood High School in 1973 and left for the University of Missouri, I knew I lacked the talent required to put on the pads at Mizzou. One of my teammates, Pete Blake, got a full ride to play for the Tigers. He was a Parade All-American and entertained offers from all the major schools including Southern Cal, Notre Dame and Alabama. Yep, even legendary Coach Bear Bryant wanted Pete. When I was a freshman at Mizzou, Pete introduced me to some of his teammates. After one look at those behemoths, I knew I'd be better suited to competing in the classroom. This wise decision paid off later but I always wondered if I could have competed at a smaller school instead of settling for intramurals and knocking around the touch leagues for years. I suffered from an inferiority complex when I compared myself to my coaching peers at North.

Coach Jon Mueller, the Offensive Coordinator, started at quarterback and punter for the Crusaders in 2001 and 2002. Jon also played baseball and basketball at Lutheran North. From there, he went on to Concordia College in Seward, Nebraska where he played football and pitched for the baseball team. Jon was recruited as a QB but injured his shoulder and wound up playing wide receiver. As a former wide receiver and QB, he was pass-happy, like me. This led to an interesting dynamic for our staff. Jon served as the Athletic Director at LN in addition to coaching football and baseball. It resulted in the odd situation where Coach Simmons reported to Jon as his AD but Jon reported to Brian as an assistant football coach. For lessor people, this could have led to problems.

Coach Simmons favored a simple, double-wing formation with a run-first mentality. Coach Mueller preferred to air it out. As a testimony to his confidence as a leader, Coach Simmons delegated much of the authority for offensive planning and decision-making to Jon. In a nod to Brian, Coach Mueller incorporated the wing formation into the mix and allowed for a heavy dose of runs with the jet, zone runs and dive plays but otherwise resembled a mad scientist akin to Mike Martz during the Rams' glory days as the Greatest Show on Turf. With our wide-open circus, we often lit up the scoreboard. It spoke volumes to me that these fellows, at the opposite ends of the offensive spectrum, collaborated to achieve success that, at times, was eye-popping.

On the other side of the ball, there was Coach Josh Cody, another youngster who handled the defensive line responsibilities. Josh served as the heart and soul of the team with his boundless, infectious energy. Like Jon, Coach Cody played for the Crusaders as a joyful, menacing, marauding D-lineman. He played defensive end at the University of Tennessee-Martin where he also excelled. I think it's fair to say, Josh could have made it in the NFL if he were a few inches taller. Coach Cody was an asset to the team. He always made our practices lively and competitive and injected a lot of spirit into the team on game day. Josh wore his emotions on his sleeve, including his openness about his faith. He never shied away from the opportunity to provide a faithful, unabashed witness for our Lord and Savior, Jesus Christ.

Josh was no stranger to hardship. He worked lots of hours at QT, all around the clock, but didn't fail to squeeze in time for the team. Josh came to many practices and games operating on little to no sleep but never lacked enthusiasm. Sometimes he caught a cat nap in his car and then jumped to life for a game like the *Energizer Bunny*. He set a good example as someone who had high aspirations but wasn't afraid to start out on the lower rungs for a chance to climb the career ladder of success.

He related to the challenges that faced some of our kids because he overcame some difficult hurdles. Josh's dad, Tony Robinson, was a star quarterback who set numerous records at the University of Tennessee and later played QB for the Washington Redskins. Unfortunately, he couldn't handle the success and got into trouble with the law and served multiple prison sentences for forgery and drugs. Josh never knew his dad. His father wasn't there to see as Josh blossomed on the football field and as a man. This was never more evident than on September 2, 2010 when Josh and his UTM teammates played Tennessee in Neyland Stadium where Tony Robinson set so many records. Josh wondered if his biological father sat in the stands somewhere peering down on him.

Coach Troy Fehrs, our resident theologian, was the polar opposite of young Josh Cody. More than their 20-year age gap, Coach Fehrs' temperament couldn't have been more different than Coach Cody's. By and large, Coach Fehrs served as peacemaker and the conscience of our team. Typically soft-spoken and thoughtful, if someone got bent out of shape about a bad call by an official, Coach Fehrs considered the other guy's position before passing judgment. Maybe it came to him naturally as a small-town Nebraska boy. I think it had more to do with his sincere faith and in-depth knowledge of the Bible. In spite of his mild mannered approach, I soon learned not to question Troy's competitiveness. When something set him off, he turned into a Tasmanian devil and the decibel level shot up like a rocket. Despite his patience and understanding, as a stickler for detail, Troy couldn't tolerate sloth, apathy or recidivism. You might cross the line once or twice to no effect but watch out if you repeated the same infraction again.

Our coaches had great football pedigrees. Coach Fehrs, played football, basketball and ran track in high school in Norfolk, Nebraska. Then he played wide receiver at Concordia College in Seward, Nebraska like Coach Mueller. Kelvin Austin, one of my Hawk buddies, was born in 1987, a year before my youngest child, and got an early start in football with the Florissant Raiders and Junior Hawks before becoming a running back for Hazelwood Central. Kelvin did a JUCO stint with the Mesabi Range Norsemen before heading to NCAA Division 2 powerhouse, Northwest Missouri State University. As a running back for the Bearcats, he helped them win a national championship in 2009, his junior year. As a senior, he almost repeated this feat while helping the Bearcats to the national semi-finals where Minnesota-Duluth edged them17-13.

Coach Lorenz, another young guy in his mid-30s, was an interloper of sorts. He played for our arch rival, Lutheran South, in high school. His Lancer past behind him, the maroon and gold coursed his veins since 2003. Like Coaches Mueller and Fehrs, he played football for Concordia College in Seward, Nebraska but the similarities stopped there. Not a pretty boy receiver like them, Mike toiled as a fat boy, as we affectionately referred to linemen. Coach Lorenz was a funny guy. First of all, as an art teacher, he seemed out of place for a rough and tough football player. His voice really set him apart too.

When I first heard him barking out commands at practice, he sounded like an Eminem wannabe. After a while, I figured out that his urban, hip hop affectation actually revealed his country boy roots. Mike, a South County boy, originally hailed from Perry County, the heart of German-Lutheran country. As the real deal, Coach Lorenz didn't trace his roots back to the 'big city' of Perryville. Although small, Perryville seemed a booming metropolis compared to his nearby home town of Frohna, MO. I got a kick out of Coach Lorenz's spirited exhortations. It made me think, *this is what Flavor Flav would have sounded like if he came from somewhere out in the sticks instead of NYC.*

We had another fat boy in the coaching ranks in Matt Hieke. A fellow Hawk like Kelvin and I, he played lineman for Hazelwood Central before he moved on to the college ranks at Culver Stockton. Though many years apart, we shared a common thread: our Hawk pride.

Coach Mike Williams and I served as the staff's old geezers. He helped me keep from feeling too out of place. Mike, once a star running back at St. Louis University High School, went on to play football at St. Louis University. Sometimes the other coaches liked to poke fun at us, claiming that we wore leather helmets when we played. Mike took some good-natured ribbing over the fact that SLU no longer had a football program. Even when he played, it had already been relegated to a club sport. Mike pulled double duty as a coach while serving on the St. Louis County Police force.

Everyone on Coach Simmons' staff had an impressive football background with me being the notable exception. At least I had a state championship to my name but that was mainly the luck of the draw. Good fortune smiled in that I happened to play on a great team. Besides their knowledge of the game, two things about these fellows stood out in my mind. First of all, young and old, everyone shared a lively enthusiasm. We had a small squad of only 44 players including freshmen so there were times when bodies ran thin in practice. Consequently, it wasn't uncommon for coaches to be called into action from time-to-time. Even Mike Williams and I got into the act occasionally.

Most often it was Coach Mueller manning the scout offense at QB. He still had a good arm, a great head for the game and could run like a deer when being chased by some of our oversized linemen. Coach Hieke donned a helmet and mixed it up on the O-line when duty called. Josh Cody did the same on defense but we didn't let him wear a helmet or pads. He played like a human wrecking ball without them. Coach Austin still flashed plenty of speed and slick moves when he filled in at running back. I loved to hear him hooting and hollering on a breakaway run. We all had a blast helping out with drills but it wasn't just fun and games. It was important to the team's preparation so the kids took it seriously. This was never more evident than the time Coach Mueller sustained a serious concussion while playing scout team QB.

Although actually a volunteer, another guy we called coach, Steve Maneikis, served as our stat guy and then some. Steve had a full-time job at the Defense Mapping Agency but still found a way to attend practices occasionally. Ever present at our games, Steve Maneikis loved the sport and, in particular, Crusader football. We were truly blessed to have him as part of our crew. He's served as a master statistician who, I'm convinced, could be a fit in college or the pros. Steve kept every detail for posterity down to the jot and tittle. However, unlike nerdy numbers guys, Steve also exhibited a true passion for football. At our games, he raced back and forth on the sidelines so as to not miss a thing. He only paused to cheer on the Crusaders. I don't know if he had a football background like the rest of the coaches but it didn't matter. He was a star in his own right.

Faith, as much as impressive football resumes, permeated Coach Simmons' staff. We shared a true, spiritual connection. Most attended church regularly. We covered the spectrum from secular-leaning to hard core Lutheran. Yet, everyone held a certain reverence for the word of God. Only some led devotions but all paid attention. We encompassed doctrinal differences but cleaved to core values rooted in Scripture. Our diversity of opinion on current events didn't diminish what we held in common. This shared spiritual bond made us more than colleagues or just a coaching staff. We had a common purpose and a shared calling that bonded us together as brothers; one family.

Chapter 7: It Takes All Kinds

Although we formed a close-knit brotherhood, you could call the coaching staff diverse by today's skin deep, quota-based definition. We had 5 whites, 4 blacks, some young, some old and a mish mash of backgrounds. At a glance, the team itself seemed homogenous. We had 44 kids on the roster including only 4 whites. From a distance, I think most people may have categorized us as just a bunch of black kids with a few token whites thrown in for good measure. Could you blame people, distant and disinterested parties, if they drew such a conclusion? Especially in the wake of the Ferguson media barrage, it seemed easy for people to apply worn out stereotypes.

Fortunately, for me, it was impossible to make such a mistake. After getting to know people on an individual basis, stereotypes were just plain silly. Broad generalizations compartmentalized people into tidy little boxes with separate categories for everything: rich and poor, young and old, male and female ... and black and white. These were shallow, meaningless distinctions.

Take the black and white labels for example. It didn't help to categorize people on the basis of skin color. What did it really tell us? If you thought it was somehow important, wouldn't you want to use a more fine-tuned gauge? Look at the Crusaders. We weren't really 40 blacks and 4 whites. My skin color certainly wasn't white. Even in winter it was more light brown or beige. In summer, I tanned up pretty nice to a golden brown. When I looked at our black players, I saw a whole range of colors. Some were very dark brown but none were really black. They covered a whole spectrum of colors with some being light enough brown that I gave them a run for their melanin money in August. Skin color didn't tell me anything about our kids as football players, students or people.

Anybody who knew anything about football could tell you that it took all kinds to make a team. We needed fat boys and pretty boys. Contrary to popular opinion, football required brains and quarterbacks needed a special kind of intelligence … maybe D-linemen not so much, LOL. Some positions leaned more on strength, others on endurance and still others on speed. Quickness must be sprinkled in with power. Receivers needed great hand-eye coordination while linemen required nimble feet. Running backs needed a quick burst, lateral maneuverability and peripheral vision but wide-outs needed game breaking speed to stretch the field. It wasn't all physical either. It took a different kind of mindset, ferocity and reckless abandon to play D-line versus O-line. Kickers ... well, they were just a few bubbles off but, regardless, still needed ice in their veins to maintain composure under pressure. There were other intangibles to consider. Kickoff coverage required a great deal of courage; some might say insanity. Good punt returners exhibited steely concentration while they fielded the ball as human missiles descended upon them from every direction. To form a great team, it was essential to have certain players with phenomenal leadership qualities. The list seemed endless.

Alchemists in a way, coaches took all of these ingredients into account in creating the perfect mixture. In order to do this, a coach first recognized that every player was different. It was important to know their individual hearts and heads. What made each of them tick? We prodded some folks but needed to pull back on the reins with others. Over-confidence often proved just as harmful as timidity. We could measure size, weight, strength and speed but that didn't ensure we could arrange all the puzzle pieces in the right spots. Critically important, the intangibles required more scrutiny than physical traits. As a case in point, I recalled my high school, superstar teammate, Pete Blake. As late as his sophomore year, he still wasted away in obscurity as a woefully misplaced linebacker. Although certainly big, strong and fast enough to be a linebacker, Pete didn't have anything close to the right temperament. Once the coaches properly recognized his unique talents, they placed him on offense in key skill positions and his contributions to the team skyrocketed.

We enjoyed plenty of diversity on our team. That is to say, we had a cornucopia of personalities and a broad range of skill sets. Unfortunately, we didn't have great depth. Coaching was a lot easier if the staff had 3 talented people competing for each position. We had 44, including freshmen and sophomores, but, in truth, we didn't even have 22 football players ready to compete at the varsity level in the Metro Conference. That meant finding special kids with the talent, mentality and endurance to go both ways on offense and defense. This was much tougher than it sounded. We lacked fitness and endurance. We had very few kids that could go full out for 4 quarters on one side of the ball, much less on offense and defense. This could be corrected, to a point, through hard work but that required time and a firm commitment from the kids.

Even with everyone in top physical condition, other problems existed. Take Isaiah Holman for example. As clearly our best athlete, common sense screamed for us to keep him on the field at all times. One thing stood in the way. Isaiah didn't possess a defender's mentality; not even close. On offense, he represented an incredible talent. Isaiah possessed breath taking speed and had the unique ability to change directions without slowing down. Additionally, he could stop on a dime and then get back up to full speed almost instantly. We could play him anywhere on offense, in the backfield, in the slot or as a wide receiver. Once he got into open space, out there where linebackers and defensive backs roamed, he was lethal. All we had to do was get the ball in his hands and let him work his magic. What made him so great was that he didn't like contact. Isaiah didn't run over people. He made them miss. However, on defense, an aversion to contact was the kiss of death. So, except for emergencies, we didn't use him on the other side of the ball. Nevertheless, he was a gazelle on offense and simply electrifying on special teams.

Something else set Isaiah apart. Too often, team stars got a big head. Self-centered prima donnas, no matter how talented, did more harm than good when it came to team chemistry. Isaiah Holman recognized his talent but maintained a quiet confidence. He didn't crow or pat himself on the back. Isaiah practiced Godly humility. He let his actions speak louder than his words; a refreshing attitude in this age of hot dogging and blatant self-aggrandizement. As a team player, Isaiah took all the accolades in stride rather than playing the part of a star. The only time I saw his demeanor change occurred when he was in the middle of a rare bad game. It distressed Isaiah when he was rendered mostly ineffective for an entire half. When I talked to him on the sideline, he didn't fret because his personal stats were lacking. Isaiah worried that he had failed his teammates. Our opponents couldn't keep a good man down forever. Isaiah escaped his first half funk and helped the Crusaders persevere after the break.

Isaiah topped the marquee but the foundation of our success resided up front. The fat boys ruled even though we lost one of our best, sophomore David Knox, to injury. Although only a sophomore, we counted on Robert Brown to go both ways as a guard on the O-line and also at defensive tackle. Already a handful at 6 feet tall and 281 pounds, Robert was formidable, fearsome and built like a grown man. He struck fear in the hearts of opposing linemen. However, in person, away from the football field, he exuded a childlike innocence. Robert could be as mild mannered off the field as he was ferocious on the line of scrimmage. Perhaps he matured early as a result of his life experiences.

Among other things, he witnessed real life struggles that went well beyond any menace he faced on the grid iron. Robert's special needs brother, Bobby, was sweet, kind and innocent. After games, Bobby often came up to me with the broadest smile and congratulated me with a big, warm bear hug. His simple sincerity and effervescent joy always lifted my spirits. Robert's mom, one of our most loyal supporters, always offered an encouraging word for me and the others.

Coach Simmons, blessed with many talented players at other schools, loved to point out how he had to scratch out success with a dearth of size. He exalted gleefully that, at North, he had some boys with plenty of "junk in the trunk." Our starting offensive and defensive fronts averaged about 270 pounds that year. Patrick Stepherson, a junior and two-way lineman, stood 6 feet tall and weighed in at 275 pounds. Jeremy Bowen, a junior and our center, reached 6 feet, 1 inch in height and tipped the scales at 285 pounds. Malik Mingo, another 2-way lineman as only a sophomore, had a budding NFL frame at 6 feet 5 inches tall and 265 pounds. The runt of the litter among starters, Dajon Stewart weighted a mere 239 pounds but had a great motor and contributed on both sides of the ball. Anthony Glover, a junior, weighed in at 274 pounds. Only a freshman and what coaches referred to as a project,

Marquis Hayes already amassed 254 pounds of girth and continued growing. Devin Hart, another freshman, also weighed 254 pounds at only 5 feet, 8 inches tall. The little guys, Dulani Evans, Cacey Brown and Donovan White weighed only 216, 219 and 201 pounds respectively.

All of our starters fit the same mold as big linemen, built to toil in the trenches. However, that's where the similarities ended. Our fat boys represented an incredible array of personalities. Mingo, easy going to a fault sometimes, provided a stark contrast to Dajon Stewart, a real go-getter. Somewhat self-conscious, Jeremy Bowen overcame a lack of confidence through his eagerness to contribute on the field. Loud, proud and aggressive, Patrick Stepherson occupied the other end of the spectrum. Donovan had a serious air about him. Some of the young guys just needed a little seasoning. Devin Hart possessed a great sense of humor. Despite their broad array of differences, a common thread existed. These guys all needed motivation to one degree or another but in a variety of forms. Sigmund Freud couldn't have done a better job than Coach Simmons and his guys in navigating this maze to get the most out of our fat boys.

I left one guy out. I don't know how because senior Renell Wren stood out in a crowd. At 6 feet,

6 inches tall and 250 pounds of lean, chiseled muscle, Renell was a college recruiter's dream. He reminded me of Aldon Smith, the Mizzou defensive end who was a first round draft pick of the San Francisco 49s. The NFL defensive rookie of the year in 2011, Aldon Smith made All-Pro in 2012 as the fastest player in NFL history to record 30 sacks. Equally impressive in stature, Renell looked the part and college recruiters from major, Division 1 programs made a beeline to North to see him. So, you might think Renell would be a coach's dream. Just wind him up and let him wreak havoc on opposing teams, right? Life and football were never that simple. Renell proved to be one of the biggest challenges for our coaching staff.

Renell, naturally strong as an ox, ran almost as fast as Isaiah Holman. This created a scary combination. However, it proved more difficult to motivate him to achieve his full potential than any other player on the team. Part of the reason was that we had such lofty expectations based on his enormous talent. In any case, we still needed to figure out what made him tick to bring out the best. In some ways an enigma, Renell toyed with opponents like tossing around rag dolls when he put his mind to it. More often than not though, he fell well short of his best. A nice kid with a good heart, Renell did fine in school. Well-grounded in the

Christian faith, he cared about other people. Yet, somehow we couldn't get his motor running on a consistent basis on the football field. As coaches, he baffled us but that didn't change our high hopes for Renell's future.

I learned a few things from this experience. First, it provided quite an insight into big-time college recruiting. By and large, the recruiters from major universities didn't care about watching game films or even hearing Coach's opinion. It basically came down to physical attributes. Tall, strong, big, and fast, Renell had a NFL frame. They didn't care if he sometimes didn't grade out well on film. As a project with the raw essentials, they believed they'd be able to fix him at the college level. Perhaps they knew best and Renell too because he secured a football scholarship to Arizona State, one of the best programs in the country. I wished nothing but the best for Renell, a good person with a kind, Christian heart.

From our perspective, I learned that all the talent in the world made no difference unless coaches could bring it out. This was not to say that Renell didn't have a good high school career. He received plenty of recognition his senior year. Nevertheless, there was little doubt in my mind that he could have achieved much more if only we'd found the key to unlock his untapped potential. We continued to follow Renell's progress at ASU and figured he just might make the big time. The last we heard, some forward-looking pundits projected Renell as a high NFL draft pick someday.

One other lineman stood out for a different reason. Cacey Brown was a perfect example of the varied challenges we faced. He didn't start but earned some playing time as a junior and offered some upside for the future. Unique among our players, Cacey outworked everyone in practice. He always volunteered for the scout teams and did his best to help the starters by giving them a good look. Cacey's motor seemed to run at 10,000 rpms all the time. His enthusiasm ran high, almost to the point of absurdity. During games, I always knew when Cacey loomed nearby on the sideline. He grunted, snarled and howled like a man possessed. Such passion and intensity sometimes provided an asset on the gridiron but Cacey was a mixed bag.

His extreme highs were sometimes matched by extreme lows. If someone approached him during one of the lows, there might be unexpected results. For example, he could let fly with expletives or obscene gestures directed at coaches or teammates. At times, he was anti-social to the point where it seemed impossible to console him. Technically, we could have cut him from the team for disciplinary reasons but that would have been counter-productive. Taking the easy way out wouldn't have helped Cacey or us. All-in-all, his spirit brought indefatigable energy to our practices. Cacey also had a good heart. Once when he hurled an obscenity in my direction, Coach Simmons called him on it. Immediately remorseful, he apologized to me with tears in his eyes. Sometimes a pain, more often Down Town Cacey Brown brought a lot of joy.

As coaches, our lives consisted of dealing with challenges and such headaches just came with the territory. But many blessings abounded that made things easier for us. Quarterback Justin Baker's outstanding leadership enabled us to run a complicated offense. A lesser QB could not have handled such responsibility and pressure so well. Only a junior, J-Bay had more games under his belt than most seniors. Smart, savvy and confident on the field, Justin didn't always show his intelligence in the classroom despite having a good head on his shoulders. Nevertheless, his football leadership provided a key ingredient to our success. Like a coach on the field, he recognized where everyone should be on every play. J-Bay knew the pass routes better than the receivers no matter how many we spread across the field.

Not a big guy at 5 feet, 9 inches tall and 171 pounds, Justin possessed exceptional strength and toughness. With his rocket arm, Justin could make any throw, anywhere on the field. He got it to the intended destination with plenty of zip. J-Bay could have rested on his considerable laurels by limiting his role to QB. However, he chose to lead by example. Justin knew we needed him to go both ways and showed his grit, determination and courage by playing safety on defense. He never shied away from contact. To the contrary, if we desperately needed a stop, he invariably came up to make the big hit. It was risky to play a star quarterback on defense but, to his credit, Justin usually dished out bigger hits than he took. This inspired the other players.

Leadership came from many quarters. One of the best was a junior, Demarcus Dotson. Like Justin Baker, he played both ways. On offense, he carried the ball as a wing or lined up and ran pass routes. Demarcus contributed well on offense but he made his mark on defense. In practice, we always used him as an example in individual drills. Demarcus worked hard and concentrated feverishly on improving his technique as a shutdown cornerback. He proved invaluable in helping the younger guys to bear down and grow as players. Demarcus was more of a technician than a banger. Although a good tackler, he usually wasn't the type who came up to deliver a devastating blow. Instead, he used his speed, reflexes and maneuverability to take the other team's receivers out of the game. Most gave up and didn't even try to throw the ball in his direction.

Sophomore Brandon Sumrall didn't always set the best example with his spotty practice habits and off-field behavior but he put his admirable football skills to good use and contributed in a wide variety of ways. At first, we thought he had an attitude problem. Coach Simmons constantly jumped on his case for being late to practice, causing trouble in the classroom or forgetting his gear. As a nonconformist, he liked to set himself apart by wearing bold colored socks and flashy earrings and sporting an avant-garde hair do. Coach Simmons frequently chastised Brandon for being a pampered momma's boy. No matter how many times he found himself on the receiving end of Coach's wrath, it never seemed to sink in. On the other hand, Brandon didn't seem like a bad kid. Never spiteful, he often flashed a good sense of humor. Eventually, I chalked up his indiscretions to perhaps a lack of maturity. On the football field, he exhibited the kind of talent that made it easier to stomach his sometimes boorish behavior.

Coach Mueller joked that Brandon, an anomaly, was the fastest fat guy he knew. Somewhat chunky, he didn't have the classic build of a wide receiver and still seemingly needed to shed some baby fat.

Yet, he possessed good speed and ran exceptional routes. His most outstanding characteristic was a pair of world class hands. Brandon could pick the ball off his shoe tops or go up in a crowd. Some of his catches dazzled us. He also put his hands to good use as our holder on PATs. Brandon played defense and, when he put his mind to it, could lay the wood to opposing players coming out of the backfield. He served as a kick returner on special teams and manned the hands team when we anticipated an on-side kick. Despite being a coaching challenge, Brandon definitely had talent. I referred to him as Renaissance Man due to his many, varied contributions.

Our broad diversity of talent and rich mixture of distinct, wonderful personalities made us a better football team. Getting the best out of such a cast of disparate characters presented many challenges. Still, it provided abundant joy in mining each individual treasure trove. Our kicker, quiet, bookish Alex Diedrich, only participated on a part-time basis. With playing soccer for LN as his first priority, he had difficulty fitting in. Nevertheless, he eventually became a fixture and even set a record for the most points in a game, 11, by a kicker in Crusader history.

Bradley West and Jamal Johnson, both good if not spectacular football players, contributed on offense and defense. However, their entrepreneurial spirit and hunger to succeed in business set them apart. These guys were inseparable. As if hanging out at school and football practice wasn't enough, they also ran a lawn care business in their spare time. Once they asked me to critique a school project for business class. In it, they outlined their plans for developing their own line of urban apparel. Their business plan had a few holes in it but one thing was certain. I knew they would be successful entrepreneurs someday based on their drive and boundless enthusiasm.

We had quite a mixed bag. Ed McMurray resembled Steve Urkel. Some might say a brainy, nerdy kid had no place on the football field but we needed every able body we could muster. He contributed well on our JV team. Devion Patterson, only a freshman, occupied the other end of the skill spectrum and even dressed for varsity games. Carl Thomas, a junior and already a role model, represented the present and future. Cameron Jackson looked like the black Mr. Clean with his chrome dome. Action Jackson, a happy-go-lucky guy who made coaching fun, played wide receiver and cornerback. Nothing got him down except when he felt he didn't get the ball enough. It was tough to spread the football around since we had so many talented skill players. Nick McGrue, another great

kid and a solid player, had plenty of upside. Jacob
Johnson, an accomplished player, helped to form
the backbone of our team. As a solid citizen with
quiet confidence, he exhibited a refreshing
demeanor. Josh Robinson, a young up-and-comer,
needed seasoning but offered good prospects for the
future.

Despite a lack of game experience, Josh
Hipenbecker seemed ready to blossom with his
combination of speed, toughness and intelligence.
Josh's future as a Crusader boded well on the
gridiron and in the classroom. Terrell McIntyre
presented some challenges. Like Brandon, he often
occupied the receiving end of Coach's verbal
lashings. Difficult to motivate, Terrell was hard to
stop once he got his head on straight and motor
running. He had good size and speed. The challenge
for our coaches was to adjust his attitude to bring
out the best consistently. Speaking of challenges,
how about David Ugweje? He transferred to LN as
a junior but, in football terms, seemed like an infant.
Growing up in Lagos, Nigeria, he had no exposure
to football. Yet, he possessed excellent speed and
exceptional intelligence with the latter hard to
recognize at first because his English still amounted
to a work in progress. How could we tap into his
innate talent? If he got loose on a jet around end, he

could run all day but he didn't know the first thing about football.

David Still, a junior linebacker and running back, offered one of the biggest challenges but became one of my favorites. Incredibly shy and humble, he turned into a beast on the football field. Built for football at 6 feet, 2 inches tall and 188 pounds of muscle, David had the kind of speed that could leave defenders in the dust but he didn't use it often enough. Drawn to defenders like a magnet, David preferred to run over them rather than around them. We called him Hammerhead because of his propensity for violent contact. This served him well on defense but proved his undoing when he suffered multiple concussions. David Still, a portrait in contrasts, returned to being one of the sweetest, kindest and gentlest kids in the world when he left the football field. He constantly supplied hugs to me and others ... always spreading the love.

It fascinated me to see how all of God's creatures were so unique. Internal distinctions of heart, mind and soul were as pronounced as our physical differences. The individual reflections of our 44 players offered a special glimpse into God's miraculous, creative power. They presented so many challenges, opportunities and joys. Yet, under Coach Simmons' guidance and God's providence, we came together as one to serve a single purpose.

Temporally speaking, forming the best football team possible while growing as students, young men and members of society served as our top priority. In spiritual terms, we shared the duty and privilege of spreading the gospel of Jesus Christ while building each other up in true, Christian fellowship by the grace of God, through His precious word.

On a certain level, I despised the contemporary use of the term diversity. It was too often used as a wedge to drive people apart and separated us on the basis of meaningless distinctions like skin color, gender, socio-economic status, age and all manner of other demographics. That kind of diversity only weakened us.

True since the beginning of time, Christ said as much in Matthew 12:25, "And Jesus knew their thoughts, and said unto them, every kingdom divided against itself is brought to desolation; and every city or house divided against itself shall not stand."

As a coach, I recognized the need for true diversity in terms of talents and temperaments. But, in bringing a team together, I much preferred an old fashioned axiom, one that still appeared on our coins in Latin: E Pluribus Unum or, in English, from out of many, one. Yes, we enjoyed the blessings of 44 players, each unique in their own way and gifted with a wide array of talents and a fascinating blend of personalities. Yet, from out of many we became one team with one Lord, one faith and one baptism.

Chapter 8: Redemption

We enjoyed incredible blessings as a coaching staff and team, the band of brothers and close knit family that God weaved together at Lutheran North. Yet, we were put to the test with our disheartening 0-4 start. Many of our fans abandoned us and we received scathing, vocal criticisms from some of the parents and others in the stands who still attended our games. Did people think we couldn't hear them down on the field? We had no one to blame but ourselves since we played without heart and succumbed to fatigue and every other challenge we faced.

Scoreboards only reflected harsh reality. They didn't capture the invisible things that often carried more weight. Our first breakthrough against rival Lutheran South represented vastly more than the less-than-inspiring score of 44-33 might indicate. Our marginal victory concealed a complete turnaround for the Crusaders. For the first time, we played as a true team. Had we won by only 1 point, it wouldn't have subtracted from our newfound strength and unity. We came together as a group of players and a coaching staff in a way that bonded us with such strength, nothing could tear us apart.

Thankfully, this didn't remain static. Our new team spirit grew and thrived. It served us well from that point forward as reflected on the scoreboard but, more importantly, in our hearts and minds.

On October 5th, 2013 we squared off against the Rams of MICDS. Before we even reached their campus, we had to confront our doubts and fears. They had a rich tradition in athletics as did LN but, in recent years; they upheld theirs more successfully than we did. In some respects they became a nemesis like John Burroughs. Our lone victory over Lutheran South wouldn't mean much if we took a step backward and suffered another thrashing like the Bombers handed us 2 weeks earlier. Then we faced the stark reality represented by their impressive campus. Like Burroughs, Westminster and Priory, MICDS's campus exuded wealth and a certain majesty. LN had a beautiful campus but it lacked the sheer grandeur of our more well-to-do conference foes. If affluence equated to football success, we had no chance. Of course, no one believed that money talked on the gridiron but, nevertheless, their splendid campus tended to intimidate us. None of that really mattered though because we couldn't be denied. We didn't play our best game but improved enough to come away with a respectable 34-14 win. Viola ... we had a 2-game winning streak!

With a much needed boost in confidence, our practices took on new life. Our guys showed they wanted to get down to business. Like most good coaches, Brian Simmons didn't usually look ahead but he made one exception. He planted a seed that, as unlikely as it might have seemed to outsiders, our key goals were still within reach. Despite our miserable 2-4 start, Coach didn't rule out the possibility of winning our district and making a run in the playoffs toward a state championship. To take things a step further, he somehow made it seem inevitable. We adopted the mentality of a team of destiny.

During the worst of times, Coach cautioned the kids and coaches against giving into the vitriol hurled at us by some of our own fans. He preached the truth about fair weather fans … "They will desert you during the bad times. Then they will rush to jump on the band wagon during the good." Coach Simmons stressed the importance of team unity. He urged, "Stick together fellas … it's not about them … it's about us. We're a family."

We played our next game at home on October 12th against Principia. For perhaps the first time in 2013, we considered ourselves clear favorites. With our newfound confidence building, momentum seemed to be on our side. Still the ghosts of our past performances haunted us. Doubts lurked in the shadows ready to pounce. The memories of our demoralizing defeats hung in the distance like a faint stench. We needed to convince all the doubters and ourselves that those failures were dead and gone. As we took the long march from the locker room toward Lamothe Field, a vision struck us. Maybe it was a sign.

Somewhere along the line, someone displayed great foresight and imagination by planting seemingly ordinary maple trees around the top of the natural bowl that surrounded the football field. For most of the year, they displayed nothing more than nondescript foliage but, in the fall, when we dreamed of deep playoff runs and championships, they revealed nature's school spirit in full glory by raising their alternating banners of maroon and gold until the season ended and they dropped their colorful leaves. It gave us a subtle boost to see one golden yellow tree next to a crimson-leaved beauty with this pattern repeated around the hilltop that rimmed our field.

This vista set the tone but we realized it would take much more than the trees flying maroon and gold flags and the matching color of our uniforms to seize the day. The Panthers didn't consider themselves underdogs. They came with plenty of fight and featured an athletic quarterback who could hurt you with his legs as well as his arm. They didn't concede anything. We knew we had to earn it. North had learned our lesson. Adversity wouldn't overtake us this time. In a total team effort, the Crusaders took another step in the right direction and hammered out a convincing 49-7 win. We still had plenty of room for improvement and remained below .500 at 3-4 but served notice that day. It was time to bury those other Crusaders who started 0-4.

Although we had new life and something to prove, we faced another dilemma that was tough for a bunch of 16 and 17-year-old kids. Could we remain humble or would we become overconfident? The latter seemed unlikely considering how much work it took to buoy our spirits but stranger things have happened. Once again, it seemed we had the edge against our next opponent, Trinity Catholic High School. We worked all week to instill the right mindset in our guys going into the game. Trinity offered a different twist in 2 key ways. First, many of our players knew their players personally and, thus, it created a special kind of rivalry. We had more depth and talent but that didn't diminish their desire to beat their neighborhood rivals. Secondly, the setting was unusual for us as a Friday night affair under the lights. The Friday night lights had a way of bringing out bizarre twists and turns.

Initially, it appeared that our messages during the week hit home. Our guys came out like a house on fire and played their best half of football of the entire season. We enjoyed a 42-7 blowout at the midpoint. During halftime, as coaches are wont to do, we disavowed we had the game in the bag. We cautioned our kids against complacency. At some point they must have tuned us out or maybe it just went in one ear and out the other. The same team that so thoroughly dominated the Titans in the first half looked like we put things on cruise control in the second half. Trinity, to their credit, came out breathing fire. They fought back hard to avenge the embarrassment they had endured early on. At first, a long TD by Trinity seemed to be an aberration, just the result of a lapse in our concentration. Then a long bomb followed. We surrendered one big gain after another that led to several scores before we felt a sense of urgency. By then, the momentum shifted hard. The runaway became a real dog fight. We hung by a thread and it appeared we might actually lose. It would have been a devastating, crushing blow and could have washed all of our dreams down the drain.

Although largely the result of self-inflicted wounds, this represented the greatest challenge we faced in a game up to that point. Since we prematurely chalked up a win, it proved almost impossible to change our mindset. Drowning in our own apathy, we fueled a Titan blaze that seemed unquenchable. Panic set in but, unfortunately, it didn't motivate us. It only led to more disarray. This reminded me of Peter's story with us stuck in stormy seas and sinking as the final minutes ticked down. Trinity prepared to pull out the most unlikely of comebacks. Somehow, our team found the will to turn our panic into resolve. We squeaked out a perilously narrow 55-52 win. Even though we won, we didn't feel like victors. However, we learned a valuable lesson that carried forward.

We finally evened our record at 4-4 as we approached the last regular season game against St. Mary's on October 25th. Although we appeared to hold an edge again, we didn't give into complacency this time. Like the week prior, we faced a Friday night contest under the lights, away from home. St. Mary's possessed less talent than Trinity but held a reputation for toughness. A bunch of hard-nosed, South City kids, St. Mary's would, figuratively speaking, just as soon slug you in the mouth as look at you. As expected, St. Mary's refused to back down an inch despite having less raw talent. This time, our guys didn't let down and took care of business to preserve a well-earned 41-3 victory.

The regular season's end lacked a sense of finality. It seemed like such a long time since the Crusaders toiled in the hot sun during June practices. Coach Simmons didn't allow any time to reflect on the prior 5 months or celebrate. In Coach's world, more than a month remained in our second season. Never mind that one loss would knock us out of the competition. Our ultimate goal of a state championship demanded 5 more wins. Nothing else mattered.

To their credit, most of our guys took the message to heart and bought into the dream and all the hard work it entailed. This required many sacrifices. With basketball season under way, a second sport threatened to pull many of our footballers in another direction. This included key players like Renell Wren and Brandon Sumrall. For some guys like Cameron Jackson, basketball represented their first priority. Although a talented football player, Cameron was even better at basketball. If the truth be known, basketball occupied first place in the heart of our star football player, Isaiah Holman. Nevertheless, our players, including these important leaders, didn't let basketball or anything else distract them from their commitment to getting the job done.

Our junior varsity players suffered the toughest dilemma at the end of the regular season. As victims of the numbers game, the JV squad never received as much attention during practice as the varsity. Most often, they had to toil in the shadows as part of the scout teams to help the varsity prepare. We barely had enough guys to fill out the JV roster and it showed during their games. In spite of a yeoman's effort by Head JV Coach Mike Lorenz, we absorbed one demoralizing loss after another. Not only did we have too few kids but we had to pull talented freshmen and sophomores up to the varsity level to plug the gaps there. By the end of the regular season, the JV kids just wanted to move on. So, it was quite a sacrifice for them to forego basketball or other interests to continue to serve as fodder for the varsity. Some dropped away while others remained faithful to the cause.

Playoff time allowed every team to hit the reset button. With regular season records tossed out, everyone started over at 0-0. Higher seeds like Lutheran North wanted to re-establish momentum and dominate. The lower seeds, the underdogs, dreamed of an upset. Crazy things often happened in the second season. It seemed fitting that our first game fell on Halloween, October 31st, 2013. Would the ghouls and goblins come out to help Herculaneum trip up the Crusaders? We didn't buy into such nonsense. From a coach's standpoint, Halloween celebrations and parties presented the greatest distraction. For us, as Lutherans, it helped to remember that October 31st marked a much more solemn and spiritually uplifting occasion. Some 496 years before in Wittenberg, Germany, Martin Luther posted his 95 Theses on the church door there and set off the Reformation that restored the gospel and helped to make God's word available to the masses. With that as our backdrop, Lutheran North prevailed with a solid 44-7 win.

Practice took on a new challenge in November with daylight a scarce commodity. Determined to get our work done, we surrounded the practice field with cars so we could fine tune the Crusader machine under the glare of their headlights. We breathed rarified air. Only 64 teams made it into the tournament in each class. Already down to 32, we needed 1 more win for a chance to play for a district title and move forward in representing Class 2. The sternest test yet stood in our path.

At 10-0, the Brentwood Eagles had their sights set on a perfect season and a state title. To make things worse, we had to play at their field on Wednesday night, November 6th. On a cold, wet evening, their field became a mess. It seemed this might work to their advantage in potentially neutralizing our speed. With their stands full and a rabid crowd behind them, Brentwood stalked the biggest win in their greatest season ever.

In a hard fought contest, the outcome hung in the balance until the final seconds ticked away. The

Eagles gave a good account of themselves but the Crusaders came out on top 26-20. Their admirable performance provided no solace to Brentwood's players or fans. Something went awry as the teams lined up and exchanged handshakes at the 50 yard line. I'm not certain what ignited the situation but a near-melee ensued. A few of Brentwood's players, apparently too distraught to shake hands, took a knee at the 20 yard line. After shaking hands with the others, a few of our players approached the ones who declined. I don't know if they wanted to console them or admonish them for poor sportsmanship. In either case, the host players took exception and some words were exchanged. Some of Brentwood's parents and fans saw this and charged our guys with blood in their eyes, hurling disturbing threats.

They made the mistake of attempting to take out their grievances, whatever they may have been, on Coach Cody. Not one to back down, I'm convinced he would have taken on the whole crowd. For a moment, it looked like the situation might descend into bedlam. A scrum formed to where one ill-advised shove or punch thrown could have led to a riot. Thankfully, cooler heads prevailed and we averted disaster by shooing the Crusaders onto the bus for a quick departure. With him still riled up, we worked to calm down Coach Cody. Thankfully he responded to reason when we cautioned that getting suspended would mean no trip to the district final the next week. Once on the bus, everyone's good humor returned and we celebrated for a short while until Coach Simmons, always looking ahead, turned the focus to our next opponent.

We played for the Class 2, District 2 Championship between Lutheran North and Carnahan on a Monday night, November 11th, at Gateway High School's field in the city. The best thing I could say about this neutral location was that it had an artificial turf field that offered a good surface on a wet night. Otherwise, the location favored our opponent due to the proximity of Carnahan, a South City high school, to Gateway. As a member of the Public High League, Carnahan mystified us a bit. The PHL was noted for its talented players but usually didn't feature the kind of disciplined teams that went far in the playoffs. However, the scores from their first 2 playoff wins, 60-24 and 62-20, indicated they had a potent offense. Beyond that, we first needed to overcome less than ideal football conditions due to the bitter cold and stiff, blustery winds that whipped across the field. Early in the game, the rain turned to sleet and later to ice. Before our turnaround and coalescing as a team, this might have discouraged us. Now, we welcomed adversity and stared it right in the face. The rain, ice and certainly the Cougars could not deter us that night. We thumped Carnahan 49-8 and claimed a district crown.

We were so close to a trip down I-70 east to the Dome. Every high school team longed to make it to the Edward Jones Dome, the home of the St. Louis Rams and site of the Missouri State Championships. Only 2 steps away, things took an about face. We enjoyed some home cooking at Lamothe Field on Saturday, November 16th. Instead of the inner city kids, this time we faced off against a bunch of farm boys from Caruthersville, MO. This represented a whole different ball game. Lacking tremendous speed and quick strike ability, our adversary featured a bunch of big, sturdy lads who liked to run the ball down their opponents' throats, churning out 4 yards here, 5 yards there and marching methodically down the field while controlling the clock. We needed to strap our helmets on tight and play big boy football. Could we, a team more akin to finesse than smash mouth football, stand up to the challenge? In a word, yes. We stood toe-to-toe and slugged it out. Our combination of speed and power helped us prevail 56-41.

We had the Dome in our sights. All we needed was to squeeze by Lamar and we'd be on our way down I-70 east. Lamar, located near Joplin, MO featured a bunch of big, tough, farm boys like

Caruthersville. That's where the similarities ended. The Tigers of Lamar appeared even bigger and stronger. Their kids seemed to live in the weight room. They possessed more than just size and strength. Loaded with speed at the skill positions and well coached, the Tigers had claimed the last 2 state championships in Class 2 football in 2011 and 2012. Watching film of their games showed that we would have our hands full.

Different than anything we had faced, Lamar featured a run-first offense where they packed everything in tight. Lamar's double wing, double tight-end package was the polar opposite of our spread. It consisted of 5 linemen and 2 tight ends, flanked closely by 2 wing backs. Their backfield contained 2 quarterbacks which seemed counter-intuitive to the standard concept of a lone field general. They fed opponents a steady diet of counter plays which meant they snapped the ball to one QB or the other who usually spun in a full circle. The ball could be handed off to one or the other wing back that came in motion counter to the direction the QB turned. Sometimes the QB kept the ball and cut up field behind the block of the other QB. Other times, the QB handed off to the other QB. We watched this different but simple approach over and over again on film and mimicked it with our scout team in practice.

We prepared well so that Lamar didn't surprise us. They carried out the same plan in person that we reviewed all week. However, our preparation lacked a key ingredient. We couldn't execute like they did. Their offense operated like a Swiss watch. They ran their well-oiled machine with such precision! One couldn't help but admire them ... unless you suffered on the receiving end. Initially, the weather didn't deter our good spirits on a cold but clear, dry day. Lamar won the toss and got the ball first. Our defense stepped up and stopped them on a 3 and out. On our first possession, it looked like we could move the ball at will. We fired on all cylinders ... until the wheels came off. Uncharacteristically, our sure handed receivers dropped a couple of easy passes that would have produced first downs and kept our drive going. When we stalled, it felt like someone let the air out of our tires. On the Tigers' next possession, they broke through for a long TD run and the rout was on.

From there on, we didn't catch any breaks. They all seemed to go against us. Lamar didn't get lucky though. They made their breaks with talent and hard work. The Tigers got us down and didn't let up. They poured it on and before we knew what hit us, the game hurtled out of our reach. I hate to admit it but they broke our spirits. I suspect that the bone chilling wind seemed much colder to us than them.

They conducted a football clinic that day. We figuratively packed up our bags early and just wanted the final gun to sound. The Crusaders couldn't find a chink in their armor until finally, thankfully, in the fourth quarter Isaiah Holman scored a long TD that gave a fleeting hint of what might have been. By the end of the game, the only thing as bitter as the piercing wind was the final score; Lamar 70, Lutheran North 7.

Maybe it was a good thing that Lamar left no doubt about who was the better team that day. It crushed us to come so close to the Dome only to fall flat, 1 game short of glory. But, at least, we didn't have to mull over any woulda, coulda, shoulda scenarios. I think it also helped our psyches that Lamar went on to win their third state championship in a row by crushing a very good Lawson team 42-0. We licked our wounds and our spirits rebounded quickly. The inglorious end to our season didn't take anything away from what we accomplished. Looking back to the dog days of summer, we still enjoyed an unbelievable ride. Given the perspective of the longer view, we had so much for which to be thankful.

Our season almost didn't get off the ground. It proved much worse than even our 0-4 record indicated. However, God had such a marvelous way of turning difficult things around to serve His good purposes (Romans 8:28). We were much better off than if we had achieved a perfect record. We had to stare in the mirror and accept full responsibility for our early failures. Full of ourselves, we originally thought that talent alone would win the day. When the season started, we weren't really a team. No, if the truth be known, we represented a bunch of selfish individuals seeking personal glory rather than team success. And, due to our stubbornness, it took 4 demoralizing losses before the truth sank in. The adversity we faced turned out to be a great and wonderful blessing.

The 2013 Crusaders came together as a team in a way that otherwise would have been impossible. When everyone else abandoned us and our fans hurled insults from the stands, it drew us together to seek shelter and refuge. We learned the value of hard work and faith. Our whole season served as an object lesson in redemption. On the football field, we all looked to something greater than ourselves. First, we looked to each other and formed a special bond. Then we cemented that bond with something more powerful than anything we could muster individually or corporately: the word of God. We received real life and power in the gospel we shared in devotions and prayers. God blessed the Crusaders with a unity that could not be severed by any outside force, not even the dark clouds of racial animus that collected across the land.

We lost our final game in a miserable fashion and fell just short of our goal of making it to the Dome. However, that couldn't take away from what happened over the course of 6 months. We came to more fully appreciate the truth that we had been redeemed, not just as a football team but as lost sinners bound for hell. We shared more than an amazing turnaround from 0-4 to an improbable 9-game winning streak. Our final, season-ending loss didn't detract from what we came to more fully understand as the greatest blessing we all shared. That is, we marveled in our common inheritance as brothers in Christ. It's captured in Hebrews 9:15 and 1 Peter 1:4 ... "And for this cause he is the mediator of the new testament, that by means of death, for the redemption of the transgressions that were under the first testament, they which are called might receive the promise of eternal inheritance. To an inheritance incorruptible, and undefiled, and that fades not away, reserved in heaven for you." This became the legacy of the 2013 Crusaders.

PART TWO – 2014

Chapter 9: Always in Season

I wish I could tell you that things returned to normal for me. With the football season over, did I continue my regular pursuits of writing books and chasing after my then 4 grandkids. This occupied a good portion of my time but football work remained. It couldn't be stored away for a year like decorations after Christmas. I learned that, in addition to being a demanding, full-time job, coaching football amounted to a year-round endeavor. It stretched well beyond practices and games.

This included season-ending duties like collecting, cataloging and storing away uniforms and equipment. A certain sense of finality accompanied some of these activities, like organizing and pulling off the team banquet and awards ceremony. However, other duties carried over from one season to the next and created a seamless continuum for coaches. This was especially true for head coaches. November to early February encompassed the recruiting season for seniors. It went beyond Renell Wren as a Division 1 recruit. Several players had the chance of moving on to the next level, albeit at smaller colleges and universities. A head coach could serve as an advocate for his players. This required time and preparation.

Counseling extended beyond just college recruits to those who didn't have a shot at playing organized ball after high school. As for college bound footballers, all of the guidance and salesmanship a coach could muster were useless if the kids didn't meet academic standards. Prodding and encouraging them to focus on school work didn't stop when the football season ended but represented an ongoing responsibility. Some didn't make it despite the best efforts of coaches, teachers and administrators. For those kids, a good coach helped them seek the next best alternative, such as a stint in junior college to get their academic house in order.

Beyond football, as caring coaches, one's attention couldn't be limited to players that might make it to the next level. Coaches prepared all the players for life as productive members of society. Consequently, we never stopped extending our guidance and support to everyone in excelling in the classroom.

Cynical coaches might conclude after the season, *hey, I'm done. These kids have to make their own way from here on out. They're not my problem anymore.* Thankfully, Coach Simmons didn't have any such cynics on his staff. The coaches liked nothing better than when kids came back years later, happy and successful, due, in part, to their football experiences. This meant much more than a championship trophy collecting dust somewhere.

As for underclassmen, this included players that didn't have much of an impact on the team, even the JV team. Still they warranted our attention because they represented the future. Standouts like Isaiah Holman and Renell Wren graduated, along with our kicker, Alex Diedrich. Thankfully, we only lost a few seniors. Most notably, Cameron Jackson, Bradley West and Jamal Johnson moved on. We enjoyed considerable success in 2013 with a very young team. This seemed to bode well for the future. Yet, gaps existed and needed to be filled with some young, rather inexperienced players in 2014. This required much time and attention to prepare the young guys to take on more responsibility. This included work in the weight room, clinics, film study and fitness training. It also meant toeing the line in the classroom. Any academic casualties just created more holes to fill. Every form of offseason preparation required some oversight from the coaches.

Although blessed with a lot of returning starters, filling our vacancies through the rebuilding process required an influx of new talent. There were strict rules against recruiting players from other schools. Within those guidelines, the coaches helped market Lutheran North. We couldn't just sit back and wait to see who came out for the team in June. Coaches reached out to interested students. This could be someone new to the area with a multitude of choices between the public school system and various private school options. A coach could assist in selling Lutheran North as the best choice from an academic, athletic and spiritual standpoint.

Isaiah Holman's graduation created the biggest hole we had to fill. Carl Thomas, a budding star and the most likely candidate, represented a different type of talent that required a few adjustments to our offense. Gifted running backs like Jacob Johnson, David Still and Nick McGrue ran the gamut of styles but none possessed the same game-breaking speed and elusiveness as Isaiah. Could we survive with a running back-by-committee approach without having a pure speed burner in our stable? We were solid at quarterback with Justin Baker returning for his senior season and seemed stacked across the line with all of our big guys back except for Renell. Plus, we looked forward to the prospect of Big David Knox coming off his knee injury. Still painfully thin even if we hadn't lost anyone, we needed about 10 good, new players to have an adequately deep squad. Facing that unlikely prospect we needed to make due again with lots of 2-way players. Even with that, a few key injuries could derail us. Heaven forbid if we lost Justin Baker. There was no one near his skill or experience level to step in if disaster struck. What would we do for a kicker? We didn't have any good prospects who wanted to pull double-duty and take time away from soccer.

Coach Simmons, a tireless worker driven to succeed, met these and other challenges head on. He faithfully kept the team together, added to it and developed everyone to compete at an even higher level. Coach also focused on his staff and preached that the coaches needed to improve too for the team to reach new heights. We attended clinics and received a steady diet of film study. We also underwent mandatory training required by the Missouri State High School Athletic Association (MSHSAA). To maintain my status as an approved coach, I had to take a course in CPR/AED/First Aid. The fact that I was certified in CPR through a course I took when I worked at Anheuser-Busch didn't count anymore. Too much time had passed and the technology curve left me in its dust. It wasn't enough to learn about chest compressions and such. Most schools were equipped with Automated External Defibrillators, so we had to learn how to start hearts back up the new-fangled way. I likened it to cranking up a car with jumper cables.

The more I learned, the more I gained newfound respect for the dedication and hard work required of coaches today. That aside, I had my own problems with which to contend. Despite the challenges of being an old dinosaur, I thoroughly enjoyed being an assistant football coach at LN during the 2013 season. In some ways, it made me feel 20 years younger. Seeing the hard work come to fruition and helping young, high school kids grow and develop was extremely rewarding. However, as the season receded in the rear view mirror, I had to face up to some harsh realities. I spread myself too thin. Football ate into time normally reserved for my other passions: writing, occasional business consulting and being a grandpa. Additionally, the rigors of coaching left me with some unpleasant reminders that I was no spring chicken.

I loved being active with the kids in practice. With our small squad, the coaches enjoyed lots of opportunities to get involved in drills and scrimmages. Joining in was incredibly fun but there was a price to pay. I enjoyed throwing the ball to our receivers the most. Once I got the old rag arm warmed up, I still tossed the rock pretty well. Unfortunately, a nagging rotator cuff tear barked at me and sometimes left my arm sore for days. I had a blast running and moving around too but, the next morning, I felt like someone sprinkled sand in my hip joints.

I also had to contend with the sun. It felt great being outside but my old skin took a beating. Sometimes I didn't notice anything until it was too late. I tanned up pretty good so I didn't think about it much but it took a toll over time. A dermatologist advised me that the season-long exposure left me with a couple of basal cell carcinomas and lots of pre-cancerous damage spots. This required me to apply fluorouracil over my entire face, twice a day for 3 weeks. The first week didn't bother me. The next 2 left my face devastated. Fluorouracil was like an external chemotherapy treatment. It attacked the damaged cells and caused them to flare up and created angry, red splotches everywhere. When I looked in the mirror, it made me realize how much damage I'd suffered. I looked like one of those zombies from the *Walking Dead*. Basically, I stayed home because, when I went out, I feared that I might scare little children.

Stuck in the middle of winter when the weather can be so depressing, I was torn by an internal tug-of-war. My enthusiasm for football battled it out with health concerns and the reality I wasn't suited for such a young man's game. Maybe the pendulum would have swung the other way during springtime optimism but, in the dead of winter, practicality won the day. After much soul searching, I penned a formal letter of resignation to Coach Simmons. I thought surely he would understand. It appeared so at first. He offered his official acceptance while expressing his reluctance. I had mixed emotions but knew it was for the best. In time, the pangs of separation would settle down. It didn't mean I couldn't be a fan. I'd still be able to follow the Crusaders, from a distance.

I should have realized that nothing was ever that easy with Coach Simmons. He never gave up without a fight. Frankly, I didn't understand his reluctance. In all honesty, I afforded moral support more than anything else. When it came to football knowledge, play calling or any other practical measure, I didn't stack up to the other coaches. The Crusaders wouldn't skip a beat without me but he didn't see it that way. Apparently, he weighted the importance of intangibles heavily. He followed a typical Simmons strategy and didn't waste a lot of time trying to debate with me. Instead, he bided his time and played upon my emotions. Coach Simmons sensed my weak spot. He knew full well that my motivation had nothing to do with money.

Coach realized I loved football and primarily did it for the kids. Knowing where his leverage existed, Coach waged a stealth campaign to get his way. He put several bugs in my wife's ear to enlist her on his side. Then he goaded some of the kids to send me emails to ask me to reconsider. Two of them, from Jeremy Bowen and David Knox, really hit home.

Between wily Coach Simmons, Bonnie's prodding and the kids, I didn't have a chance. My heart warmed up to the idea with the weather as April rolled around. The end of the school year approached quickly. It wouldn't be long and we'd be launching the 2014 Crusader campaign in June. How could I not get excited in thinking about all of our returning lettermen? If I didn't know the kids personally, things would have been different. Unlike a bunch of nondescript football players, they were a joyful gaggle of individuals, each with their own story and unique personality. I guess Coach had me pegged all along as an old softie. I missed my coaching buddies and the players: my surrogate brothers and kids.

I couldn't abandon them, so I rationalized that I would handle things differently. There would be less throwing to benefit my bum shoulder. I'd buy a hat and plenty of sunscreen. Realistically, I loathed hat head and didn't have the discipline to use greasy sunscreen regularly. Also, I would never deprive myself of the simple joys of coaching by cutting back on running and throwing. However, there were some positive changes in the offing. With a year under my belt, my grasp of the play calling improved with all of our passing routes committed to memory. With the roster of returning players' names mastered, I grasped a better understanding of how things worked, including the schedule for practices and game day routines. My second year promised to be smooth sailing compared to my rough start in 2013. I just needed to find a way to squeeze everything into my schedule: writing, grandkids and football. Once I made up my mind, I was all in.

Chapter 10: Diversity Run Amok

Any notion that we could easily pick up where 2013 left off died rather quickly. Even though most of our starters returned, many new challenges and opportunities confronted us. The players changed so that we couldn't plug them all into the same slots. Only Justin Baker proved the exception since he had already matured physically and mentally as our field general. Many others grew and filled out, making them look all the more like serious ballers, ready to roll. This included Brandon Sumrall, Robert Brown, Malik Mingo, Jeremy Bowen, Patrick Stepherson, Terrell McIntyre, David Glover, David Still, Donovan White, Jacob Johnson, Cacey Brown, Josh Hipenbecker and Nick McGrue. Though still small in numbers, we had a solid nucleus of big, fast and talented players. Despite these blessings it still left us with some glaring needs.

David Knox represented perhaps the biggest addition, literally and figuratively. A large individual, David stretched almost as wide as he stood tall. After suffering a devastating knee injury the year before, he came back in great spirits. David possessed a big smile and personality to match his hulking body. We really needed him considering our general lack of depth and the loss of Renell Wren. As a junior, David was ready to fill a big hole in the line and any void in leadership. Although extroverted, David avoided being too brash. He led vocally and by example. He played with a lot of fire but, off the field, behaved like a gentleman, polite and respectful. David and Robert Brown served as massive bookends who anchored our line. They provided quite a handful for opposing lines along with Patrick Stepherson whose size matched his tenacity. Jeremy Bowen had grown even larger and tipped the scales at 300 pounds. The big, quiet man came into his senior year with newfound determination. Could we develop our other big guys to round out our line play: Malik Mingo, David Glover and Donovan White, among others?

Question marks remained regarding who else might step up and provide depth in practice, in games and on special teams. Dulani Evans had excellent speed for his size but lacked aggressiveness. What did we need to do to ignite him? Terrell McIntyre looked like a football player but needed to improve his focus. Perhaps with a little seasoning and more repetitions, he could be a frontline player on the line or at linebacker. Could we harness Cacey Brown's unbounded energy and enthusiasm? As a senior, Josh Hipenbecker looked ready. Not the biggest guy, he was plenty strong and determined. Josh also had a good head on his shoulders and it showed in the classroom. Perhaps he could fill a void at linebacker. We needed to take advantage of his speed.

We had a solid nucleus and some good prospects among our returners. However, we suffered some of the inevitable subtractions beyond the seniors who had graduated. Marquis Hayes was somewhat soft and apathetic as a freshman but had towering stature. Unfortunately, we didn't get a chance to tap into his sizable potential since he transferred out. Perhaps our best up-and-comer, Devion Patterson, also transferred. This hurt our secondary and depleted our depth further. He had a good football build and mentality. As a freshman, he gained some varsity experience in practice and in games on special teams. We also lost Dajon Stewart, a guy we counted on to make major contributions on the defensive line. Dajon had good size and speed and a great motor. James Myers, a young guy and somewhat of a project, had good upside. Unfortunately, we didn't get a chance to nurture his potential since he left the squad. Some of the other guys who didn't come back were not necessarily noteworthy losses based on their youth, inexperience or past performance but, to us, every loss detracted from our already questionable depth.

Thankfully, we had some pluses to offset some of the minuses. Chance Wyatt, painfully thin, possessed plenty of speed. In addition, he fancied himself a kicker, something we sorely needed. As a young, inexperienced player, we didn't expect Chance to have a major impact but he gave us more depth. DJ Henderson came out for football and, in spite of his diminutive stature, looked like he could add to our mix of running backs. Solidly built and strong for his size, DJ knew how to seek positive yardage. Unfortunately, this experiment never came to full fruition. DJ left the team in mid-season. Although small compared to Robert Brown or David Knox, Andy Gordon and Jesse Guffey possessed adequate size and were scrappy. Both made solid contributions in practice and helped spell some of the big guys from time to time during games. They also contributed on special teams. Jesse, better known for his baseball prowess, fancied himself as a receiver. I ribbed him by calling him Skinny. He assured me he had good speed but had put on weight since breaking his ankle during a baseball game. This proved to be accurate. He wound up working himself into the offense as a tight end in certain formations.

Devin Hart wasn't new but he seemed like a different guy as a sophomore. Short and rotund at over 250 pounds, he didn't quite look the part but there was a football player inside of him. I likened him to a little Warren Sapp. Devin caught our eyes because he could stand his ground better than expected against behemoths like David and Robert during practice drills. I enjoyed having him around because of his youthful exuberance and good sense of humor. He kept things light and fun. In spite of his laid back, jovial demeanor, his football skills stood out. Once we threw him into the action, he displayed a quiet ferocity in the trenches.

We didn't expect much from Daniel Gilmore despite his senior status because he hadn't played football with us before. Lots of guys have reached the big time after a late start in football but we didn't see Daniel Gilmore as a rags-to-riches story. He reminded me of Chance Wyatt with his slender build but he had speed to burn. He ran as fast as anyone on the team but could he catch the ball? He surprised us in two ways. As the year wore on and we experienced some injuries and other issues within our normally deep receiving corps, Daniel stepped up to help replenish our ranks. More importantly, he revealed great, God-given faith. Like Bradley West the year before, Daniel took it upon himself to lead team devotions and prayers on many occasions. His leadership provided an unexpected blessing.

There were other guys who weren't quite ready to make their mark on the varsity level but flashed enough potential to grab our attention. These guys helped the starters improve by giving them a good look on the scout team. With any luck, some of them could even work their way onto special teams and get some varsity reps by the end of the season. Kyle Goldman, a tall, lanky receiver, might give defensive backs a fit once he honed his skills. Jordan Howell and Andrew Parker were ballers who just needed to develop over time. If we squinted, we could envision young Chase Martin as a serviceable receiver someday. Andrew Bolstad lacked obvious football skills but possessed great determination. He had the kind of mindset that could prevail by his senior year, once he grew and filled out. John Smith, Ryan Smith and Keyshaun Van Dyke, diamonds in the rough, seemed like the types that would eventually make their mark at LN, just not in 2014.

Additions offset some of the subtractions but we needed some guys who could step up pronto. Thankfully, some exciting new talent surfaced that had an immediate impact. As a natural athlete, sophomore Jordan Sommerville's youth didn't matter. Being Justin Baker's little brother, he had great bloodlines. Jordo, fit right in as someone who could play backup QB, run the ball, catch the ball and, most importantly, help shore up our defensive secondary. A runt of a freshman at maybe 125 pounds, soaking wet, Martize Jenkins looked like another natural. Fast and shifty, Martize was so small that opposing defenders had difficulty seeing him behind our massive offensive linemen. Despite his diminutive stature, he didn't shy away from pounding the ball inside. Freshman or not, we made room for Martize on the varsity because of his fearless attitude. Motivating him in the classroom proved to be our biggest challenge with Martize.

With all the changes, one thing remained the same. We hadn't filled the gaping hole left by our star, Isaiah Holman. Our fortunes turned when Cortez Simmons transferred to Lutheran North. No relation to Coach Simmons, Cortez represented both a blessing and a curse. Though blessed with undeniable talent, Cortez differed from Isaiah in some key areas. He wielded explosive, breakaway speed like Isaiah but lacked his shiftiness. Cortez had great moves and could be elusive but didn't have Isaiah's ability to dart to and fro on the fly without slowing down. However, Cortez Simmons possessed a more solid build. He boxed competitively and, at times, his pugilistic mentality came out. He didn't shy away from contact.

Whereas Isaiah always tried to make you miss, sometimes Cortez dropped his shoulder and lowered the boom. The complete package, Cortez could run and catch and was an electrifying kick returner. He could also play defense in a pinch but preferred to operate on the other side of the ball mostly.

Was he a coach's dream come true? Unfortunately, this big bundle of talent came with a downside. At times, Cortez exhibited a terrible attitude. He often didn't apply the brains God gave him as well as he could in the classroom. Coach constantly harped at him to toe the line. It seemed Cortez put forth the minimum effort necessary and no more. Cortez's problems stretched beyond the classroom. His poor attitude leaked out onto the football field too. At times, it seemed like there were two Cortez Simmons. One day he would be happy and cheerful. I got a kick out of the way he returned kicks in practice. On good days, he toyed with the scout team and weaved his way through would be tacklers with ease and giggled and chortled along the way as he sprinted for a touchdown.

When Cortez had a bad day, everyone knew it. He refused to talk to teammates or coaches as he walked to the practice field. If anyone dared to greet him, he rebuffed them with grunts, growls and scowls. No one could talk him down off his self-imposed ledge. He kept the details of his problems to himself. From what I could gather, he had problems on the home front that often ate him up inside. His family faced financial issues too. Cortez remained an enigma. Although one of our most talented players, he gave the coaches more fits than anyone else. Sometimes he skipped practice citing some lame excuse. If we threatened him with a game suspension, he showed up at practice only to be felled by some mysterious injury. We eventually learned not to play his game. Like with the little boy who cried wolf, we had to ignore his feigned cramps, hamstring pulls or faux concussions in practice. Invariably, he experienced a miraculous recovery and returned to practicing at full-tilt, if and when it suited him.

At times, we wanted to just write him off. We had other talented players that weren't so temperamental. We'd miss his skills but, at times, it didn't seem worth the effort and headaches necessary to draw him out of his gloom and doom dungeon. Something about Cortez told us not to give up. Not a bad kid, he could even be delightful on those days when his dark moods dispersed. If only we could help Cortez triumph over his evil twin! Could we find the key to unlock this mystery before our patience ran out?

Our concern transcended Crusader football in that we wanted Cortez to reach his full potential as a person. One day I asked him what he wanted to do after high school. I envisioned him as a scholarship athlete gaining a good university education. He declared dismissively that he just wanted to work on cars. Exasperated, I told him to aim much higher. I said that, if he wanted to work on cars, he should set a goal of owning a large chain of auto repair shops. Cortez sort of shrugged off my suggestion but something in his eyes told me he at least entertained the possibility. I hoped that he found encouragement in the fact that we recognized his full potential.

Cortez represented the highest pinnacle or lowest depth possible for the Crusaders in 2014. Thankfully, we had other options. We had a solid core of gifted players ready to step up and take the lead. Demarcus Dotson could man the slot and run the jet or stretch the field on deep pass routes. Most importantly, he had the ability to anchor our secondary on defense. As a senior, he had matured into a true, shutdown cornerback. As a leader, we turned to him in practice to show the younger guys how to run drills properly to hone their skills. Almost a sure thing, we knew we could count on Justin Baker for results and leadership on both sides of the ball. Only a junior, Brandon Sumrall still lacked a bit of maturity but helped lead us on the football field. He developed into a clutch receiver that put his fabulous hands to work for us time and again. Brandon also contributed on defense until a shoulder injury limited his playing time.

Nick McGrue, Jacob Johnson and David Still rounded out our talented group of seniors. They had matured physically, emotionally and spiritually to the point where they bore a good portion of the load in 2014. They all served as 2-way players who contributed significantly on offense and defense. Nick, Jacob and David reflected the foolishness of stereotyping people. Without knowing them, one might draw all kinds of erroneous conclusions. Judging from the way they competed on the field, there could be a tendency to label them as typically dumb, shallow, Neanderthal football players. Nothing could be further from the truth. They played with reckless abandon and didn't shy away from violent contact but, off the field, offered a different view. Jacob, in his dark, thick-rimmed glasses, maintained a rather studious image in the classroom. Happy-go-lucky Nick, the tough football player, was ever so gentle and caring around his sister who suffered with a serious illness. Old Hammerhead, David Still, would knock you silly during a game but otherwise proved as kind, gentle and soft-spoken as could be. All of them possessed an abundance of faith in Christ.

All-in-all, we enjoyed a mother lode of talent despite only having 40 players on the entire squad, including freshmen. We suffered more defections and losses due to injuries and such but had some late additions too. Coaching football was a mercurial profession. Change was constant and we either adapted quickly or failed. With our 2014 campaign still ahead, we had no time to ponder the unknown future. Open slots had to be filled. Most notably, we didn't have a kicker. All of the talent in the world might go for naught without a decent kicking game. Many times, extra points, occasional field goals and special teams play made all the difference between winning and losing. We had a wealth of diverse talent with a good combination of size, speed, tenacity, smarts and leadership. However, we weren't quite diverse enough. How could we be a good football team without someone to put a foot to the ball?

We enjoyed plenteous diversity in the variety of talents our kids possessed and our rich cultural and ethnic mix. Although still predominately black, we added 3 more white kids and even went international with 2 players from Africa and another from China. Lutheran North was blessed to have a fantastic international outreach program. We had 20 international students attending North in 2014. This amazed me considering LN's small size. It reinforced my view of the quality education and atmosphere Lutheran North offered. Additionally, it evidenced how God worked in any setting, regardless of size, to accomplish His good purposes.

I found it astounding that some of our international students came out for football. That they overcame the language barrier was tough enough but it amounted to more than just mastering English. Football had a language all its own and the terminology sometimes perplexed even those with the best command of the English language. We had guys like Daniel Gilmore who followed football from a fan's perspective most of his life. Yet, he struggled to make the adjustment as a first-time participant. I couldn't imagine trying to bridge that wide divide with a language barrier to boot. This proved too difficult for one of our African students, James, despite being a gifted athlete. The other, David Ugweje from Lagos, Nigeria, made the transition. Although lost from a tactical standpoint, he persevered to where he made a number of worthwhile contributions. He even scored a few touchdowns in JV competition. David delighted us by setting a great example, behaving like a gentleman and exhibiting a positive attitude. He also shined in the classroom.

Jackson Ye blew away the stereotype of Chinese people being small. Jackson had a lineman's build, stood taller than Robert Brown or David Knox and wasn't far behind in girth. As only a freshman, it looked like he might grow into quite a lineman. Jackson faced a real struggle due to the language barrier and his total unfamiliarity with football. However, his biggest drawback was his mild temperament. During one JV game, he came over to me on the sideline with tears in his eyes. This big, hulking guy whimpered about a much smaller opposing lineman who slapped him upside the helmet. I tried to fire up the gentle giant to return the favor but failed due to his meekness. Later during the season, I asked him how to say the word angry in Chinese. It took a few violent hand gestures and ugly facial expressions to get my point across but, eventually, it sunk in and Jackson said, "Shengqi de." That's how it's spelled but his pronunciation sounded like shun tee to me so that's how I said it too. From that point forward, I had a lot of fun with Jackson on this. Whenever I felt he needed a boost of aggression, I'd thump him in the chest; get right in his face and growl, "Shun tee!" He just smiled and laughed like a big, jolly panda.

Our cornucopia of diverse talent didn't change the fact we still had no place kicker. Coach Simmons started working on this dilemma at the

end of 2013 when Alex Diedrich completed his
eligibility. He scoured the school looking for a
hidden gem. Finding another soccer player to split
his time with us represented our best hope but,
unfortunately, we found a bare cupboard. No able
bodied boys on the soccer team had the time or
nerve to brave the gridiron. Coach Simmons put his
imagination to work in a way that caused diversity
to run amok. He mentioned his hair-brained scheme
during the off season but I thought he was joking.
Surely he would pull a rabbit out of his hat by the
time June rolled around.

We started our first practice of 2014 with warm-
ups and stretching. Then we broke down into our
normal groups for individual drills. The running
backs went with Coach Austin. Coach Heike led the
O-line and Coach Cody guided the D-line. I
normally tagged along with Coach Fehrs who had
the defensive backs and wide receivers unless he
worked with the special teams. Troy told me I could
work on my own with the kickers to start things off.
I took this as a vote of confidence from Coach
Fehrs. That is, until I strolled over to where our
place kicker stood around looking rather aimless. I
must admit that I was shocked. From a distance, I
might not have noticed but, up close, in spite of the
pads and helmet, there was no mistaking that

something was very, very wrong. Our kicker was a
… girl!

In a near panic, I realized that Coach Simmons
had not been joking. Were we that hard up for talent
that we had to break a cardinal rule? This really
bothered me. I had learned a lot of new tricks in
2013 when the other coaches helped me to fast-
forward into 21st century football but, in some ways,
I was still a dinosaur. I considered myself pretty
progressive when it came to gender equality but,
doggone it, football was supposed to be the last
bastion of masculinity! I worried that having a girl
on our team, even a kicker, made us a laughing
stock. My head almost exploded. I mustered every
ounce of tolerance, tact, diplomacy and self-control
at my disposal to approach her civilly. I introduced
myself and she told me her name was Karsten
Klotzer. *Oh boy*, I thought, *we're not only stuck
with a girl but she has a crazy name that's hard to
pronounce.*

I guess I feared she might be some kind of
female, high school activist, out to make a name for
herself. Right off the bat, I got a different picture.
She certainly wasn't pushy. In fact, she seemed
almost as out of place as I did. Karsten didn't have
an agenda. She had volunteered at the behest of
Coach Simmons. We had a need and she was brave
and willing enough to try to help out. Her motives

seemed pure and I could tell this was harder on her than anyone else. Sensing her predicament, I quickly shifted into coach-mode. I thought to myself, *just do your job. We don't have a kicker. Can this girl boot the darned thing through the uprights?*

She had her helmet off while we talked. I couldn't help but notice her long, blond, braided ponytail. I remarked, only half in jest, about cutting off her braided beauty or tucking it inside her helmet. This solicited a worried but very emphatic response advising me that Coach Simmons had promised her she could keep her ponytail. This spoke volumes and revealed something that became more apparent later. Karsten, understandably a bit timid and lost given her completely unfamiliar surroundings, didn't lack courage. She didn't fear taking a stand on principle. I noticed the pink headband she wore to keep her hair in place and the sweat out of her eyes. Her initials, embroidered in fancy, script letters, appeared to read KKK. The shock must have registered on my face because she questioned me in an animated, concerned fashion. "What's the matter? Why are you looking at me like that?"

I somewhat sheepishly suggested, "You might want to get rid of that headband."

"Why, what's wrong with my headband?"

"Don't you think your teammates might get the wrong impression?"

"Why, what's wrong with my initials?"

"Your initials are KKK?"

Karsten busted out laughing. "It's KRK, Coach. My middle initial is R."

I got a good laugh out of the misunderstanding too but still added, "From a distance, that squiggly R looks a lot like a K. Have you got another one you can use instead?"

She smiled, "I've got you Coach." From that point forward, Karsten usually sported a Mizzou headband which suited me just fine.

After our comical icebreaker, we focused on the business at hand. Somehow my resistance to football feminism melted away. We had other problems though. Karsten didn't have a clue about football. She was a fan but playing the game was another matter. The task at hand seemed monumental because she didn't know the first thing about place kicking, not even the simplest basics. So, we started with very rudimentary essentials such as where to place the kicking block in relation to the goal posts. I served as the holder while she took aim and gave it a try. Initially, she didn't even know how to line the thing up or where to make contact with the football. I tried to maintain a positive attitude. I thought, *well, maybe there's a silver lining. At least she's not starting out with any bad habits.*

As we proceeded, Karsten's ability to adapt to her new, peculiar surroundings pleasantly surprised me. I should have known that Coach Simmons did his homework on Karsten. As I found out later, she had an impressive background as an athlete. Known primarily as a star on the soccer team, Karsten also excelled as a cross country runner. She performed well on the basketball court too. As a natural, gifted athlete, Karsten succeeded at everything she tried. Still, at first, it was a little hard to picture her as an accomplished athlete. She was fit and well-conditioned but small for a girl. Karsten didn't fit the part of a rough and tumble tomboy. She looked more like a cute, adorable, girly girl. Without her pads and helmet, most people would have pegged her as the girl next door rather than a football player. She liked it that way too. She treasured her ponytail and had all the interests of a regular, high school girl.

As a football player, she proved very coachable. Karsten took instruction well and caught on quickly. Once she got the hang of things, she demonstrated

good mechanics and plenty of leg strength. Coach
Simmons had uncovered a gem. Karsten wasn't the
type of kicker who could boom kickoffs into the
end zone but she had just what we needed on extra
points: reliability, consistency and an unshakable
constitution. Coach Fehrs referred to her as K-
Money. I labeled her Special K. I shed my objection
to a female gridiron incursion and learned to truly
appreciate Karsten's presence on the team. She
possessed a great sense of humor and a refreshingly
honest outlook. Never intimidated by the boys,
Karsten had no problem calling them out when she
felt they were out of line. I laughed at the irony
sometimes. Karsten hung with the boys in the
manliest man's world, football, but never sacrificed
her femininity. She wasn't fazed by onrushing
linemen bearing down upon her or kickoff returners
who might run over her. Her biggest worry seemed
to be her hair. She hated what the helmet did to her
golden locks … too funny!

Something else seemed ironic about having a
girl kicker. The Crusaders featured a bevy of
talented football players, some of which were bound
for glory at the next level. Highly ranked, North
returned a host of starters from a team that made it
all the way to the state semi-finals in 2013. Yet, the
media didn't take much note of us, except for our
girl kicker. Karsten brought more media attention to

the Crusaders than anything else we might have accomplished on the football field. This didn't generate any jealousy because Karsten remained unassuming and unselfish. The coaches and players took it as a plus that she garnered some good press for us. Yes, diversity had run amok in our football program but we didn't mind at all. We delighted in the fun of having Karsten around. Additionally, she helped us to watch our manners much better than we normally did by dispensing with some salty language and other indiscretions usually found around the gridiron. Most importantly, we felt thankful for a kicker that could put the ball through the uprights on a consistent basis.

Chapter 11: Poised for Liftoff

The 2014 Crusaders seemed in a better position to succeed than the year before when we wound up 1 game short of our goal of playing at the Dome. With a year under its belt, the new coaching staff under Brian Simmons came together as a dedicated brotherhood with a shared passion and goal. Although we banked on some juniors and sophomores to play major roles, we had a wealth of seniors and many of our underclassmen had some solid game experience. We found a new star, although a sometimes temperamental one, in Cortez Simmons. Although a small squad that lacked depth, the Crusaders possessed plenty of experience, speed, talent, size and leadership. This was especially true in key positions with players like Justin Baker, Carl Thomas, Demarcus Dotson, Robert Brown, David Knox and Brandon Sumrall. We even filled the glaring hole left by our departed kicker, Alex Diedrich, with, of all people, a cutesy, little, blond girl with a bright smile and nerves of steel.

A haunting question remained though. Could we avoid stumbling out of the starting gate like the year before? Could we improve our conditioning enough to prevent wilting in the summer heat during our first few games? Other critical concerns bubbled just below the surface. Which Cortez Simmons would show up in practice and on game day, Dr. Jekyll or Mr. Hyde? Would we dodge the bullet and avoid devastating injuries to key, irreplaceable players like Justin Baker? Would everyone take their school work seriously or would eligibility become an issue? Would we get full of ourselves and admire our press clippings or remain humble and dedicated? Most importantly, could we go about the business of football while keeping our priorities in order with God and family taking precedence?

With these things top of mind, we came together as a team and committed to getting better every day. This group showed dedication from day one but an unspoken fear haunted us. No matter how well our season unfolded, our bogeyman, Lamar, still stood in our path to the Dome. Lamar embarrassed us on our home field to bring 2013 to an end. There was no reason to believe they wouldn't be just as formidable in 2014. We didn't dwell on it but Lamar represented the ever present elephant in the room. This served a good purpose as long as it didn't distract us from our day-to-day work. It provided a constant reminder that we needed continuous improvement in order to achieve our highest goal.

We adopted a pragmatic approach as we prepared to launch our 2014 season with 2 months of summer practices. With the playoffs 5 months away, a seeming eternity, dwelling on Lamar made no sense. The prospect of other challenges loomed much closer: failing grades, injuries, poor attitudes and other day-to-day hardships. We felt well prepared to overcome these obstacles and any adversity that came our way. We were poised for liftoff as the start of the school year approached in early August. However, something totally unprecedented happened that posed a much greater danger than anything we ever envisioned. It put our whole season in jeopardy. Would we shoot for the moon like Apollo 11 or plummet to earth like the disastrous Challenger and Columbia Space Shuttle missions?

We withstood the tragedy, controversy and racial tensions created by the death of Trayvon Martin in 2013. As a whole, Lutheran North withstood the immense pressure that caused great fissures elsewhere. True fellowship in Jesus Christ helped us to put this in the past without suffering underlying fractures to weaken our bonds as brothers and sisters in Christ. The perspective we shared within our personal sanctuary at Lutheran

North contrasted significantly with the world outside where many open wounds festered. Some healing occurred when the news cycle moved on but it didn't last long. New events cast salt into these unhealed sores and caused profound irritation and pain.

At first, we easily ignored the latest tragedy since it occurred in New York City, seemingly a world away from St. Louis. The date was July 17th, 2014, 1 month before the start of the regular season. In this unfortunate incident, a black man was killed by police officers while resisting arrest. While it fit the same pattern to a certain degree, the circumstances were significantly different. Eric Garner, a gentle giant of a man, committed a misdemeanor by selling black market cigarettes on a New York City street corner. Caught on video, the incident splashed across the national news. Even though it lacked the context of what led up to the incident, it was hard to justify what happened. It took several officers to wrestle the big man to the ground and one, Officer Daniel Pantaleo, applied a choke hold that apparently caused his death by asphyxiation. Any notion that the earlier Trayvon Martin incident had faded from relevance was put to rest swiftly. This roused dormant forces that connected the dots in a foreboding way.

I watched the video like everyone else. Was there a connection to Trayvon Martin? In my mind, I couldn't see it. One case, properly adjudicated, involved self-defense by a private citizen. The other appeared to be excessive use of force by the police. I didn't want to rush to judgment in this situation, despite the compelling video evidence. Perhaps key elements of the story eluded the camera. One couldn't deny that Mr. Garner resisted arrest but could it have been handled differently? Many jumped to conclusions before the investigation ran its full course.

I still had faith in our judicial system. However, many people in our country had some strong doubts. I could sympathize with them in this particular instance. Although Mr. Garner failed to comply and resisted, the encounter seemed relatively mild and it didn't appear that he posed a significant threat to anyone. Granted, I wasn't on the front lines when they fought to bring the mammoth man under control. Still, it seemed excessive to me and his death was certainly unnecessary. Did he have a violent past or a rap sheet filled with other, more serious crimes? Did the officer have deadly intent or did another contributing factor like poor heart health claim Mr. Garner's life?

Judging from anecdotal evidence, it seemed like most people felt the police used force gone awry. Yet, most people appeared willing to let the system play out. However, another much smaller segment of the population lost all patience. These folks connected the dots, rightly or wrongly, and concluded this reinforced the notion that police, in general, systematically subjected blacks to unfair treatment. The situation remained volatile in the immediate aftermath but then settled down when the case was assigned to a grand jury on August 19th.

This didn't distract us from our mission as a football team. Our awareness had been raised but this still seemed like an isolated incident in faraway New York. Grueling work in the scorching August heat preoccupied our minds on North's dusty practice fields. This all changed on August 9th, 2014. In some respects, it provided a watershed event in our nation's recent history. Darren Wilson, a white police officer, shot and killed an 18-year-old black man, Michael Brown. For some, this proved to be the final straw. It supplied the spark that ignited the powder keg of resentment that had built up in some quarters for quite some time. More than a simple rush to judgment, the visceral reaction happened so fast it even preceded many of the conflicting accounts that surfaced rapidly.

This time, we couldn't ignore the situation. The latest tragedy wasn't in far-off Los Angeles or New York. The shooting of Michael Brown occurred here, right in our hometown of St. Louis. To make things even more salient to us at Lutheran North, the incident didn't occur downtown or somewhere on the mean streets of North St. Louis. It happened literally in our back yard, no more than 2 miles away from our campus. Peaceful protests erupted into violence, looting, burning and vile, hateful rhetoric that engulfed the news in a non-stop, 24/7 cycle that stretched far beyond St. Louis. It garnered national and international attention.

Suddenly, the name Ferguson no longer represented a quaint, sleepy, mostly blue collar community nestled within the parochial patchwork of St. Louis County. Ferguson took on a new mantle as the hotbed of civil and not-so-civil disobedience in America. Almost overnight, Ferguson became the heart and soul of the struggle for social justice, a mystifying term with very different implications depending on one's point of view. To some, it made Ferguson famously noble like Selma, Alabama during the civil rights march of 1965. Others likened it more to the infamous Watts riots that same year.

It's fair to say elements of both existed. Some protesters came to make a point and strike a chord for positive, peaceful reform. Others appeared as anarchists bent on venting uncontrollable anger and sowing the seeds of mindless destruction. The situation quickly spun out of control. The court of public opinion jumped to conclusions and, some folks, with the help of the media, pushed a narrative that swiftly took hold regardless of a lack of proper vetting and evidence. It was misplaced and, from hindsight, erroneous but that didn't matter. It took root and propelled a movement whose bounds reached far beyond Ferguson, around the globe.

Power and efficacy wouldn't be confused with accuracy. Later, much of the narrative would be disproved by impartial eyewitnesses. However, it would be of no effect. 'Hands up, don't shoot' would become a battle cry. It would become a cause celebre where, for example, several St. Louis Rams players would employ the hands up gesture to make a statement about race relations upon their entry in front of a live television audience. The movement would even adopt a name that would become recognized around the world and ignite solidarity efforts in other cities like Baltimore and Chicago: Black Lives Matter. The movement would even impact the next presidential campaign.

Certainly, Lutheran North couldn't go untouched. It was absurd to think that our tiny little band of players, coaches, students, teachers and administrators could resist such a powerful, all-encompassing, global force. This worldwide movement, with its irresistible sphere of influence, hearkened at our doorstep. The epicenter and symbolic birthplace of this social phenomenon, the burned out remains of the Quick Trip gas station on West Florissant Avenue that had been destroyed during the riots on August 11th, was barely 2 miles from Lutheran North. We shared strong bonds at LN but never encountered something quite like this before. No one had. Who could fault us if this splintered us; something that had torn apart a nation and influenced the entire planet? Michael Brown's death and the turmoil it created in its aftermath could not be overestimated.

Our first responsibility, the safety and security of North's students and staff, fell squarely on the shoulders of Lutheran North's Principal, Tim Brackman. It was the last weekend before the start of the new school year on Wednesday, August 13th, 2014. As one might expect, the Administration and faculty had spent a lot of time over the summer in preparing to kick off another academic year. The weekend of August 11th should have been a time for everyone to relax and get their batteries fully recharged. The last days of summer were normally filled with excitement and anticipation for students, teachers and administrators alike. Michael Brown's death changed all of that. Phones blew up as calls flew between Mr. Brackman and his Crisis Team. It consisted of Dan Wenger, Dean of Students; Jon Mueller, Athletic Director; Cindy Burreson, Director of Counseling; Darin Keener, Dean of Chapel; Jane Mark, School Nurse and Byron Devrouax, School Social Worker assigned by Lutheran Family and Children's Services.

Well trained, this Crisis Team could handle a variety of situations ranging from tornadoes to fires, earthquakes and all manner of potential disasters. However, they never anticipated anything quite like the unrest in Ferguson following the shooting of Michael Brown. As virgin territory, the situation represented something much more perilous than any natural disaster. To some, Principal Brackman may have seemed ill-suited for the herculean task that loomed ahead. Tim was born and raised in the small town of Wausau, Wisconsin. At age 6, he and his family moved and settled into St. Charles, Missouri. He spent the bulk of his life thereafter in what he deemed "a vanilla existence". Surrounded by a lot of white, Lutheran folks, Tim had minimal contact with black people. He openly conceded this wasn't the best preparation to lead a highly diverse student body in dealing with a very dangerous, racially charged situation on the back stoop of North's campus.

If one unwisely judged a book by its cover, Tim Brackman didn't appear to be up to such a challenge. Although he possessed the inner toughness and character of a former athlete and coach, he lacked the imposing build or stern countenance of a man who might strike fear in his adversaries. Tim looked like an intellectual sort, generally mild mannered and prone to calm logic. Nevertheless, he stepped into the breach well prepared. One of Tim's favorite Bible passages was found in Proverbs 3:5-6, "Trust in the Lord with all thine heart; and lean not unto thine own understanding. In all thy ways acknowledge him, and he shall direct thy paths." Was there a better way to approach the unknown or a more reliable guide in navigating an unprecedented situation? Tim didn't have a diverse background before coming to Lutheran North but his heart rested in just the right place. He looked at people as individuals. Tim practiced fairness on the basis of human relations, not race relations. His well-ordered priorities placed God first. Tim put his trust in the Lord and revered God's word in the Bible as the source of authority and truth in all things.

Much the same could be said for everyone on the Crisis Team and Tim Hipenbecker, President of the Lutheran High School Association. As such, no one panicked. They avoided an overreaction or,

worse, lack of action due to paralyzing fear. Mr.
Brackman and his team developed a wise and
simple plan aimed at striking a reasonable balance
between security and normalcy. With safety
paramount, the emotional, psychological and
spiritual well-being of the students also took
precedence. This balanced approach combined
practical safety measures with trust in the Lord.
With God's edifying word and Mr. Brackman's
steady hand at the helm, Lutheran North launched
the school year on time, albeit under a cloud
emanating from the explosive events just a stone's
throw away from campus.

Coach Mike Williams, an active duty police
officer working part-time for the St. Louis County
Police, served us quite well in the ensuing crisis.
Although an important part of Mike's life, coaching
football necessarily took a back seat to his law
enforcement duties. Mike's experience spanned 35
years He graduated from the St. Louis City Police
Academy before being recruited by the County in
1978. Mike worked in several capacities and then
transferred into Crimes Against Persons in 1981
before he settled into the Drug Enforcement Agency
(DEA) in 1987. Although St. Louis County signed
his paychecks, he was attached to the DEA until
2006. This dangerous assignment involved Federal,
interstate drug trafficking. Mike worked undercover

in interdiction and intercepted drug couriers while pursuing the bigger fish up the chain of command. During his time at St. Louis University, Mike learned Spanish and this came in handy in this line of work.

In 2006, Mike transferred back to Crimes Against Persons until his retirement from full-time police work in 2012. That didn't last long. After 6 months of R&R, Mike went back to the force part-time, mostly in the Bureau of Professional Responsibility or Internal Affairs. In this capacity, Mike helped field complaints leveled against police officers and also screened potential candidates for the police force. This provided keen insights into how to separate fact from fiction regarding allegations of police misconduct and in discerning good cops from bad ones. His special skills and experience proved valuable to LN on August 9th, 2014 and thereafter. Mike served well in keeping Principal Brackman and his Crisis Team properly informed about potential dangers.

Mike's role seemed strange to me and others since we never pictured him as a grizzled police veteran and tough, no-nonsense kind of guy. We all knew he was a cop on the side but Mike kept it low key for the most part. In person, Mike was the last guy you'd peg as a cop, especially one that had worked undercover in chasing down drug pushers.

One of the most laid back and personable fellows I'd ever met, Mike's casual, friendly smile seemed permanently affixed. He was the antithesis of the kind of cops being maligned, fairly or unfairly, in the press. Mike didn't have a mean bone in his body.

To his peers at North, Mike was a coach first and police officer second. Mike coached for all the right reasons: he loved the game and cherished the kids. Mike's work with kids preceded his many years on the police force. He started as a camp counsellor at St. Louis University High School in 1971-1972. From there he coached grade school kids in basketball and soccer before turning to football at the North Side Youth Association.

In 1985, Mike was pegged by Vice Principal Kirk Mueller, Jon's dad, to handle plain clothes security details at Lutheran North. Back then too, LN desired to balance safety and normalcy by avoiding a uniformed police presence, where possible. Mike once recounted his first impression of the kids at Lutheran North, "They were so well behaved and the blacks and whites got along famously." Mike was so enamored that he sent his own kids to North. God seemed to be working all things together for good. Mike finished with his last group of 8th Grade footballers in 1999 and LN asked him to coach C-Team football in 2000. He's been at North ever since.

Mike's incredibly patient and nurturing coaching style didn't fit a cop's hard-nosed persona. Mike, admittedly not an Xs and Os expert, made the hard work of teaching the young guys the basics his specialty. As he liked to say, "Some things don't change, like proper blocking, tackling, ball handling, catching and running." I had to laugh when I heard the narrative that cops systematically mistreated and abused certain segments of the population. I couldn't help it because I immediately pictured Officer Mike Williams. A selfless guy, he always looked out for the best interests of the kids. Cross words never emanated from his smiling face. Mike's unassuming style put him at odds with the stereotypical, menacing image often assigned to police officers. Although different, it worked because Mike served as a role model as a cop and a coach.

In an incredible coincidence or perhaps a felicitous display of providence, Mike was close to the scene on August 9th. He and about 29 other colleagues arrived that morning at Emerson Electric for an annual picnic hosted by an association of black police officers. Mike's group rented a pavilion and picnic area at Emerson's headquarters situated smack dab between Lutheran North and

Canfield Green Apartments, near the site of the shooting. Colonel Kenneth Gregory hosted the picnic. Mike Williams recounted how family fun and frolic succumbed to the ever present call of duty, "Pagers went off indicating that an officer-involved shooting occurred. Shortly thereafter, we saw patrol cars streaming down West Florissant. Then we received the signal for Code 1000 which meant to send help to a situation involving crowds." Mike noted gravely, "In my 35 years on the force, I had only seen 4 Code 1000s issued." Then he added ominously, "A little while later, we received the signal for Code 2000. I had never seen one of those in my entire career."

Thereafter, Mike remained close to the Michael Brown situation and this benefited his fellow coaches, Principal Brackman and his Crisis Team. The intelligence and sound advice he provided helped the Crisis Team strike the right balance between security and normalcy. Sound judgment was put to the test right out of the blocks. Circumstances demanded decisiveness 2 days before the official start of school due to new student orientation. This added an element of uncertainty for Principal Brackman. Although he contemplated that returning students could handle the Ferguson protests without giving into fear, panic or rash behavior, new students represented an unknown quotient. Would someone react inappropriately causing sparks to fly? Mr. Brackman and his team showed courage, resolve and faith. They proceeded with Orientation as planned on Monday, August 11th. Daylight served as a worthy ally and things went without a hitch. However, as a precaution, they cut short after-school activities such as football practice at 5:00. They instructed parents and students to enter and leave campus via I-70 and Lucas & Hunt Road to avoid taking the West Florissant route.

Principal Brackman issued regular communications to parents and students on almost a daily basis. They contained practical information downloads that you might find in any other school's communications. However, the updates coming from Mr. Brackman's office reflected a different tone and tenor and offered soothing reassurances. His first memo on August 11th opened this way:

"Dear Crusader Families,

We are saddened by the events that occurred in the Ferguson area over the weekend. The awareness of the fact that we live in a sinful world doesn't lessen the reaction of our human hearts and minds to the effects of this situation on people and businesses in the area.

We want to let you know that the Lutheran North campus and the surrounding area are safe and unaffected by the incidents. We pray that this will continue to be the case. Our new students are here today, excited to join the Crusader community. We are thankful for the peace that passes all understanding as God is in our midst."

He closed in a similarly hopeful and upbeat way that you would not likely find in our sanitized public schools:

"I am happy to address any questions or concerns you have. We are thankful for the safety of our campus and for our Christian community that gathers in God's love as we grow together in Him. Lutheran North has been a stabilizing influence in our city for nearly 50 years. We pray that God will continue to work through us here at 5401 Lucas & Hunt to further His plan."

Lutheran North possessed something special that distinctly set it apart from its rancorous surroundings. The peace, safety and security we enjoyed were gifts from God. We all knew this … administrators, teachers, coaches and students … as a matter of faith. God richly blessed us, even in practical matters, through His caring, loving, guiding hand. I'm convinced that Mike Williams' presence didn't occur by accident. He was a

godsend along with our Precinct Captain, Guy
Means, who served faithfully and kept us well-
informed and safe. I suspect that even the secular
authorities sensed God's presence and providence at
North. Early on, they asked for permission to use
our campus as their base of operations. Principal
Brackman wisely turned them down. Although
sincerely grateful to the police, he respectfully
declined in order to maintain the balance between
normalcy and security.

Mr. Hipenbecker, Principal Brackman, his
Crisis Team and the entire staff at North remained
resolute and calm throughout the seemingly endless
ordeal. They never lost sight of our guiding light.
Tim Brackman provided a reassuring reminder in
closing his final communication memo on August
12th, just prior to the start of the school year:

"Recall this year's theme verse: 'Your Word is a
lamp to my feet and a light for my path.' (Psalm
119:105). God not only lights our path to salvation
but He is also using us as lights to our battered
community."

We never wavered from this course despite the
nearby nightly turmoil, anarchy and violence that
streamed into our homes via the local and national
news. Life at Lutheran North carried on as near to
unaffected as possible. Unlike many other schools,

we didn't suffer interruptions to our normal routine, other than cutting after-school activities short. That is, until August 20th through the 22nd. We didn't shut down due to the events in Ferguson. Ironically, we closed school for 3 days due to a water main break that left us without service. Perhaps this was a blessing in disguise since it gave us the opportunity to experiment with a new concept called eLearning. It worked out well enough that we really didn't skip a beat academically.

As for the football team, we didn't need tap water to accomplish our work. Nothing would delay the launch of our 2014 season. One might have expected distractions and some lively discussion as our practices continued the week following the shooting of Michael Brown. We weren't immune to the current events of the day. In such an emotionally charged environment and based on human nature, a very real possibility existed that someone might willfully or inadvertently detonate an angry, divisive, racially charged dispute. However, nothing of the sort occurred. The topic of Michael Brown came up but without any fireworks despite the hands up; don't shoot narrative that circulated ubiquitously. As a true band of brothers, everyone seemed to keep an open mind without anyone rushing to judgment.

Some of the credit went to Mike Williams who kept us well-informed with the inside scoop. Mike cautioned against jumping to conclusions. He relayed some of the information about Michael Brown's background and dubious activity just prior to his encounter with Darren Wilson. Mike once told me, "We knew right away that hands up, don't shoot never happened." Some of our coaches, understandably upset at the notion that a compliant, black teenager got gunned down by a white police officer while trying to surrender, showed proper restraint and good judgment in waiting for the investigation to play out. Coaches on the other side of the fence practiced similar restraint and waited to see whether Darren Wilson's closet contained any skeletons before rushing blindly to his defense. Collectively, we valued our friendship and brotherhood too much to jeopardize it by taking sides in the evolving, volatile tragedy involving Michael Brown and Darren Wilson.

We tended to the business of football as all of this unfolded just prior to the start of the regular season. We kicked things off as part of a 4-team jamboree at Festus High School on Friday night, August 15th. This afforded us the chance to scrimmage against outside competition and fine tune things before our first real game. It helped us to keep our priorities straight but we couldn't escape the Ferguson-effect completely. We returned to campus after 10:00 at night. Mike Williams and one of his colleagues provided security but we couldn't help but wonder if Lutheran North would remain a quiet, safe sanctuary at nighttime when the protests usually turned dangerous. Thankfully, there were no signs of trouble.

The next week proceeded without incident except for the water main break. Undeterred, our excitement mounted since it was finally game week! Our first game took place on Friday night, August 22nd, under the lights at Clayton High School. Everyone recalled how they had beaten us 34-7 at home the year before and started our horrendous 4-game skid. We had wilted in the heat and let them have their way with us in an utterly embarrassing fashion. Although a night game, the heat was still intense at 7:00 p. m. It was hot enough that the game was delayed a half hour. Their turf field seemed to absorb and hold the heat. Although confident, we still entertained some doubts. We needed to get the monkey off our back and put 2013 completely behind us. It didn't take long to put a new stamp on the 2014 season. Our new attitude was apparent from the first kickoff. We thoroughly dominated the Greyhounds in posting a 49-0 win. This offered notice to everyone that Lutheran North represented a force to be reckoned with in 2014.

The Ferguson-effect persisted. The unrest resembled the Energizer Bunny's evil twin. It just kept going and going. However, we put it out of our minds for the most part, even when we returned to campus from Clayton in the darkness late that Friday night. Again, our sanctuary place was unaffected.

That we maintained our focus was due, in good measure, to people like Mr. Brackman, his Crisis Team, Mike Williams and Captain Guy Means, along with the entire staff, teachers and student body at North. From a football standpoint, Coach Simmons deserved much of the credit for the normalcy we enjoyed. He set the tone with his staff. Coach encouraged an open dialogue about Ferguson but helped us keep our priorities in order. We concentrated primarily on meeting the needs of the kids and pursued our team goals and dreams. With our attention riveted on football, the unrest in Ferguson sometimes seemed a world away. We had achieved a successful launch but, with the Principia Panthers up next, needed to keep the ship on course.

Chapter 12: Rocket Ship

Riding sky high after our successful liftoff, our team possessed a different mindset. We eschewed overconfidence since the lessons of 2013 remained fresh in our minds. We avoided becoming lackadaisical and took our preparations seriously even though our second game seemed less than challenging. Principia didn't put up much resistance the year before and looked more vulnerable in 2014. A good number of their senior leaders were suspended due to some unnamed infractions. In essence, we faced what amounted to a junior varsity squad. As coaches, that is, natural worry warts, we feared the worst. Would the kids take this game seriously? We knew that football lore contained scads of underdog stories where David had toppled Goliath. We had to prevent such a letdown.

The defensive coaches set a goal to keep their charges focused. They wanted nothing less than a shutout, a big goose egg. What could we do to generate the same intensity on the other side of the ball? With the help of Coach Mueller and Steve Maneikis, we delved into Crusader history. The most points scored by Lutheran North in a single, regular season game amounted to 66, as amassed by the 2010 team against Lutheran South. This seemed unrealistic considering the mercy clock rule where, if one team is ahead by 35 points or more after half-time, the clock is not stopped except for injuries or timeouts. This required a team to pile up the scores in the first half to break such a record.

Undaunted, we aimed high in order to give the offense an extra incentive. The guys remained highly motivated and carried out their mission with businesslike determination. We led by more than 50 at half-time and both goals appeared attainable even if somewhat of a stretch. The clock ran and we substituted freely with backup players but the Crusaders still set a new record with 72 points. The defense held up their end of the bargain too. Unfortunately, a special teams' letdown resulted in a Panther kickoff return for a touchdown. We won going away, 72-7 but Coach Simmons was sorely disappointed. He wanted that goose egg! It provided a good lesson for the kids to never let up.

We all suffered butterflies leading up to September 6[th,] the day of our opening home game and first real test of the season. Westminster throttled us 31-14 the year before and seemed to have our number, perhaps even more so than John Burroughs. If we knocked them off, it would set a completely different tone for 2014 and solidify our pursuit of a perfect season. We ran roughshod over

Principia but then maybe slacked off. Or perhaps we underestimated the Wildcats. In either case, it became clear early on that we were mired in quite a tussle.

Coach Simmons referred to such contests as a game of inches where both teams fought tooth and nail for every tiny parcel of turf. It was nip and tuck down to the final few minutes. All appeared lost when North trailed 21-20 and Westminster had the ball with the opportunity to run out the clock with a first down. Then lightning struck. Justin Baker picked off a pass and returned it deep into Wildcat territory. Momentum switched to our side and it seemed certain we would score and pull the game out of the fire. Then everything imploded. One of our undisputed leaders and most reliable players, Carl Thomas, had trouble with the handoff on a 43-ISO run left. A wild scramble for the fumble ensued and it inexplicably bounced right up into the hands of a surprised but opportunistic Wildcat defender. He sprinted all the way into the end zone for a 27-20 win.

Devastated, our hopes for a perfect season were dashed, only 3 games into the season. It cast great doubt on North even competing for a Metro Conference crown. Worst of all, it almost broke our spirit. We failed after our first brush with football adversity. Our confidence was crushed. We should have shrugged it off and looked toward our next opportunity but guilt consumed us. I think everyone questioned our level of effort. We felt collectively that, too slow out of the gate, we let one get away. We almost gagged on the painful irony that our best player had coughed up the ball. Even indefatigable Carl Thomas landed down in the dumps. This concerned the coaches since the rest of the team depended on Carl's indomitable spirit so much.

To make matters worse, we broke a cardinal rule by looking ahead. We looked past Priory to the next week where a showdown with our old nemesis, John Burroughs, loomed. This kind of thinking could be the kiss of death. How could we prepare for a solid opponent like Priory if we were worrying about John Burroughs? We couldn't help ourselves because the Westminster defeat meant that a loss to Burroughs would knock us out of the race for the conference championship. Our minds wandered toward the possibility of an ugly losing streak. We lacked focus and that made the task of bouncing back against Priory much harder. Could we avoid falling into a complete tail spin?

Thankfully, Coach Simmons refused to let us wallow in self-pity. He figuratively grabbed the team by the collar and shook us out of the doldrums. Coach assured us in his convincing fashion that all of our goals were still achievable.

We remained in the conference race. A district championship tarried in the distance along with the state playoffs. He challenged us, "What's the point of a perfect regular season if you don't win a state championship? Let's keep our eyes on the prize!" Coach Simmons refused to let Carl Thomas stay down in the dumps. "Are you ready to give up because of one lousy fumble? We can't do this without you. Now step up and be a leader!" Carl accepted the challenge. He shook off his disappointment and assumed the mantle of leadership once again. With Carl out front, the whole team came together and readied for Priory.

We needed a good week of practice without further hiccups. That included the matter of Ferguson that continued to simmer at a low boil while everyone waited for the Grand Jury's decision. The wheels of justice seemed glacially slow as the unrest dragged on. The protesters demonstrated real staying power. How long could we avoid the dangerous distraction that constantly knocked at our back door? In my frustration, I couldn't help but think, *don't these people have jobs and other responsibilities or are they professional protesters? If so, who's paying them?* The media constantly fed the beast but, from our football perspective, we forced Ferguson into the background, that is, until September 10th.

Our friends on the police force provided a heads up to LN that the protesters planned on turning the heat up a notch by staging a shutdown of Interstate 70 at Hanley Road, just a few exits down the highway from Lucas & Hunt. This caused a concern that, if they succeeded in doing so, it would stop the flow of traffic along the safe route to Lutheran North and force people to take the more dangerous path through Ferguson along West Florissant.

I got the word that the shutdown was planned for some time between 2:00 and 3:00 p. m, right about when I usually made my way to practice. I hoped to avoid the back route since I remembered what happened when the trouble first started. I visited my late father-in-law, Les Verseman, in Christian Northeast hospital before practice. Although aware of the protests in Ferguson, I didn't expect any danger during the daytime. Thus, I opted not to drive west all the way to Bridgeton via I-270 and then back east down I-70 to LN. Why spend 35-40 minutes when I could take Lewis & Clark to Chambers to West Florissant in half the time?

This was a decision I regretted when I ran into the gauntlet near the burned out Quick Trip on West Florissant. Protesters milled about onto the street so that traffic halted with cars forced to squeeze through the crowd. Some folks actually smiled rather pleasantly as they issued their cheerful chants. Others seemed to pose more of a threat. It was hard to gauge the level of danger … but I must admit it made me feel rather uncomfortable.

With this still firmly in my memory, I thought, *damn the torpedoes*, and decided to take I-70 and braved the possibility of getting caught up in the rumored shutdown. Thankfully, I made it through unscathed. The police took proactive measures and prevented a quagmire. With about 20 squad cars parked along the highway and more on the Hanley overpass, the police made a strong show of force. I arrived at practice early and sat in my car and mused as I looked out toward the LN Athletic Complex. The tree-lined practice fields were so peaceful and serene. Lamothe Field reminded me of a Norman Rockwell painting. It offered a panoramic view of the adjacent, bucolic Norwood Hills Country Club golf course with its lush, rolling fairways. Further off in the distance, the soccer and baseball fields stretched all the way to I-70. One disturbing aspect marred this otherwise perfect slice of Americana. That glimpse of nearby I-70 reminded me of our world gone mad.

As I drank in the tranquility surrounding me, I marveled at the amazing contrast presented by our stark surroundings. It seemed the world truly had come unhinged. A painfully long month had passed since the shooting that launched days of intense unrest and wanton destruction, yet nothing had really changed much. Every night, the nearby stretch along West Florissant became a virtual war zone. It was not safe or prudent to venture into that section of Ferguson late at night. As we often cautioned our players; nothing good ever happened after midnight. We foolishly expected things to settle down, especially in light of the revelations regarding the original narrative. A security video revealed that Michael Brown and his accomplice, Dorian Johnson, stole cigars and menaced the shop keeper in the process. Additionally, other facts unfolded that challenged the notion that Michael Brown tried to meekly surrender with his hands upheld. Still, the anger, resentment and, in some circles, racial animus persisted.

It bothered me personally that St. Louis and Ferguson in particular received such a black eye. The images strewn across the TV on a daily basis misrepresented the city I had known and loved all my life. I wondered, *what is this doing to local residents and businesses? Property values must be plummeting. Mom and pop enterprises must be barely treading water. It served no purpose. Would something good come out of this? Was there healing in the offing? Could this somehow unite people?* The exact opposite appeared to be the case. Sometimes I reconsidered. Perhaps an underlying problem existed, some terrible injustice that needed to be addressed. I realized some peaceful protestors had noble intentions. However, this didn't excuse the savage behavior of anarchists who controlled the night. It served no good purpose to burn, loot and spew blind hatred. I just couldn't reconcile the two.

This conundrum reinforced my belief that you shouldn't judge a book by its cover. I shuddered to think how my perception could have been shaped if formed solely by the images splashed across the TV. Thankfully, the media didn't dominate my point of view. I learned some important truths by being up close and personal. Take Terrell McIntyre for example. A late bloomer as a football player, Terrell matured right before our eyes. The dire situation in Ferguson helped me understand why he had problems keeping his head in the game. Terrell lived in Canfield Green Apartments, right near where the fateful shooting occurred. He was the product of a very tough environment and it amazed me that he turned out so well.

I also realized that Ferguson was more than the war zone depicted on TV since it produced a fine young man like Terrell. He was part of the neighborhood but never got caught up in the trouble or violence. To his credit, Terrell's mindset was focused strictly on getting to school and football practice. He was stuck smack dab in the middle of a neighborhood that most people avoided like the plague. However, it didn't affect Terrell in a negative way.

During the first 2 weeks of unrest, he stayed away from home with a couple of teammates so he could make it to school unimpeded. Otherwise, Terrell remained unaffected. He rarely mentioned the Ferguson situation except for the time he asked if we could practice at Rams Park in Earth City since McCluer North enjoyed that privilege. I laughed at the way he approached Coach Simmons. He noted correctly, "We're a lot closer to the trouble in Ferguson than they are." I imagined the warped opinion I might have held toward Terrell if not for our personal friendship. As a book, Terrell McIntyre was a great read in spite of his rough cover.

Terrell's tough circumstances reminded me of Dulani Evans. Dulani asked me for a ride home from practice on several of occasions. He lived within a few short miles but in the other direction, south down Lucas & Hunt, not far from Normandy High School where Michael Brown once attended. The first time I dropped him off, it surprised me that one of our guys lived in such a blighted neighborhood in a tiny, weatherworn house. As a public school kid, I thought mostly affluent students

attended private, parochial schools like LN. I grew
up in a lower middle-class, blue collar family. As a
baker's son, I joked that we were white collar since
my dad wore a white uniform covered in flour dust.
Engrained in my youth, I maintained the notion that
only rich kids could go to a private school. Terrell,
Dulani and others helped to bury that misconception
for good.

Many of our students came from nice, middle-
class homes. Some enjoyed a fairly affluent
lifestyle. But others came from broken homes and
bad neighborhoods, constantly mired in financial
dire straits. It didn't matter though. They excelled
despite their circumstances. They appreciated the
opportunity to get a good education in a safe,
nurturing, spiritually uplifting environment.
Perpetually upbeat, Dulani, like Terrell, didn't use
his standing in life as an excuse for low
expectations or failure. He dreamed of pursuing an
appointment to the U. S. Naval Academy in
Annapolis, MD. Dulani's determination convinced
me that he would either wind up at Annapolis or
some other institution of higher learner. One thing
was sure. Due to Dulani's exemplary attitude, I
rooted for him to succeed and fully expected him to
become part of the next generation of our nation's
leaders.

My ponderings ceased as school let out and players streamed from the locker room. Practice went off without a hitch despite the diversion created by the threatened shutdown of I-70. By the grace of God, the commotion made us stronger and prepared us for the adversity still ahead. Dealing with distractions seemed to help us sharpen our focus on football. It made us a more disciplined team.

Football provided a welcome contrast to the abstract world of social rhetoric and political posturing that radiated from Ferguson. Football relied on unambiguous results displayed plainly on stark scoreboards. We were relieved to get back to the simple, enjoyable basics of football. Still fate offered another wrinkle to make things a little more interesting. The school moved our game on Saturday, September 13th back to 2:00 to accommodate all the seniors that took their college entrance exams that day. This provided an altogether different distraction but it didn't matter. We came together as one and dispatched a worthy Priory team 61-27.

Our rocket ship returned to our original course just in time as we headed into an asteroid belt. Just ahead stood the Bombers of John Burroughs who had thoroughly embarrassed us 69-35 on our home field in 2013. We didn't engage in a lot of rah-rah talk during practice. We didn't need to say a word since everyone keenly recalled the pain they inflicted upon us. With the emotional scars still raw and the team already motivated to a fever pitch, Coach Simmons didn't dwell on the past by dredging up unpleasant memories. With the Metro Conference race at stake, we needed a win to stay in the hunt with the hope that Burroughs might knock off Westminster. The 2014 schedule favored us with a second consecutive home game against the Bombers. I think some of us secretly wondered if this accrued to our benefit or disadvantage. The thought of suffering defeat at Lamothe Field in front of the home crowd was dreadful.

Our home field advantage didn't dampen Burroughs' confidence. Undefeated and ranked number 1 among area small schools by the St. Louis Post-Dispatch, they had every reason to feel self-assured. Apparently, one of their players had a birthday on September 20th because they came prepared for a party. They cluttered the visitors' sidelines with all the necessary fixings including a banner, big birthday cake and bright balloons. This didn't escape our attention. After vanquishing us, they apparently planned more than just the normal football festivities. We thought the Bombers planned to rub our noses in it with a birthday celebration right under our noses on Lamothe Field.

Could you blame them? They whipped us badly the year before, featured a great quarterback and returned an unstoppable, superstar running back in John Moten who shredded us with ease in 2013. They represented a star studded, experienced, well-coached outfit. Still, we couldn't stomach the perceived disrespect and cockiness we felt their party plans displayed.

During my time at North, we witnessed some great play by stellar Crusader athletes. However, I'm sorry to say we rarely played a full game. Even when we won big, we usually suffered a letdown in at least one quarter. Coaches always looked for their team to have their best game, especially when the stakes were high. The two biggest games we played in 2013 reflected dismal failures. Our losses to John Burroughs and Lamar left us utterly humiliated. While those two great teams deserved much credit, some of the blame rested with North. We offered two of our most uninspired, mistake-prone efforts.

September 20th, 2014 proved altogether different. The Crusaders fired on all cylinders from the opening bell and never let up. We didn't just compete ... we dominated. In the biggest game to date during my tenure, our guys produced their best football by far. They executed almost flawlessly and displayed great vigor and spirit. We toppled the number 1 ranked Bombers in a rousing 53-30 victory. Thinking of their audacious birthday party plans, I snidely recalled Marie Antoinette. When food riots broke out among the starving peasants during the French Revolution, it was reported that she infamously said, "Let them eat cake." This wasn't a fitting attitude for a Christian but it was hard to rein in the emotion in the heat of the moment.

Drubbing John Burroughs and shutting down their superstar, John Moten, provided quite a rush. It meant more to us than just a football game. It restored our hope of at least sharing in a conference championship. A win over such a highly rated, defending champion validated us. It helped erase the melancholy that lingered from the Westminster loss. Most importantly, it strengthened the bond we shared. We set our minds on something highly unlikely, if not nearly impossible, and prevailed magnificently. It was a product of hard work but, more importantly, faith … faith in each other and, ultimately in our God. When asked about their most memorable recollection of our 2014 season, players invariable recounted the victory over John Burroughs. This victory meant just as much to the coaches. It showed us that the kids listened and took our lessons to heart. We were proud fathers on that day.

We faced more adversity than anticipated at such an early juncture. We found some in the hallways and classrooms of North. At times, it seeped into our practices. It enveloped us in a dark cloud on game day against the Wildcats. Football aside, it had us surrounded. We did well in weathering the Ferguson storm but it never relented. It rested on our doorstep. It lurked on Interstate 70 and invaded our living rooms nightly through our televisions. It seemed endless and inescapable. As Dan Wenger, our Dean of Students, so aptly put it, there may have been 7-10% of the student body who were attuned to the protests or wanted to follow what they considered a movement. However, the other 90%+ just wanted it to go away. They wanted to move on with their lives as normal teenagers and students. As a football team, it was even more lopsided. Every last one of us wanted to focus solely on the task at hand. The Burroughs game showed us coaches that our team was well-equipped to do just that. With hearts and minds in the right place, our rocket ship charted a steady course and entered a lofty orbit.

Chapter 13: Inspiration

We confronted an odd situation in coming off our momentous victory over Burroughs. We faced a troublesome, almost inevitable letdown with our next foe since Lutheran South represented a perennial loser on our schedule. This was inexcusable since South's prospects improved with the addition of an exciting, young talent, Cody Schrader. We cautioned our senior-laden Crusader team not to underestimate the freshman. Film revealed that Number 7 repeatedly ran wild for South out of their backfield and made key plays on defense too. Still, some of our guys may have tended to discount him since we had virtually owned the Lancers for many years except for 2012. That it was an away game added to what shaped up as a formula for disaster.

Many teams suffered letdowns after big wins. Thus, coaches invariably trotted out that tired but true cliché about playing one game at a time. Every game offered a different challenge. One week's accomplishments counted for nothing the next. South cared little about our victory over Burroughs. On Friday night under the lights at their house, they enjoyed the advantage of a spirited, hungry crowd behind them. Like most years, the Crusaders dreamed of running the table and winning a state title. South needed only to whip us to make their season. Regardless of other factors, one thing clearly favored the Lancers: motivation.

Although less than imposing at 5' 9", we learned quickly that Number 7 packed a punch. He carried a load of talent in a small package. As the game wore on, seemingly meaningless intangibles amounted to large obstacles for us. The raucous crowd instilled great confidence in South. We found ourselves with a real fight on our hands from more than just Cody Schrader. The home faithful fired up all of the Lancers. When the dust settled at half-time, we held the short end of the stick.

When we came out after the break, the mood in the night air was palpable. With our heads laden with doubt, the Lancers seemed sky high. South picked up where they left off and, by the time the fourth quarter rolled around, we stared at a deficit of 15-14. We faced the real prospect of a devastating loss that could negate every good thing we had gained against Burroughs. As the clock wound down, our doom seemed more and more likely. We desperately needed something to shake us up. Who could provide the spark we needed to turn things around? The answer, or at least part of it, came from the most unlikely of places. We couldn't get our offense untracked, so the defense needed to pull our fat out of the fire. We asked our defense to not only stop the other guys but come up with a score too.

Although an incredibly tall task, they did just that and not once but twice. The old and new guard combined to pull off a stunning family affair. The brothers, Justin Baker and Jordan Sommerville, the veteran leader and the new kid on the block, produced back-to-back pick 6s. Each of them intercepted a Lancer pass and returned it for a Crusader touchdown. Just scoring supplied more than enough drama but they added icing on the cake. Justin and Jordan both orchestrated thrilling, long returns, darting and dashing, weaving wildly through South's would be tacklers in a dramatic fashion that brought the Crusader faithful to their feet.

With disaster averted, we all breathed a sigh of relief and then the celebration ensued. J-Bay took it all in stride as just another in his long string of accomplishments. As for Jordan, he enjoyed some rarified air that served as a harbinger of things to come. As Justin and Jordan were interviewed by local TV sportscasters, we watched with delight. Relief and joy abounded on our happy ride home. We all took pride in seeing them featured in the online version of the Post-Dispatch. As for the coaches, we were particularly satisfied to see one of our rising young stars step into the big shoes left by some of his predecessors.

The thrilling victory aside, adversity never seemed far away from Lutheran North. The Ferguson-effect rarely encroached on our football sanctuary but we felt its presence elsewhere on campus. Consequently, as students, our players faced some of the same dangers, fears and frustrations that touched their schoolmates. Although a safe place where normalcy prevailed in spite of the tumult surrounding LN, nagging doubts persisted since the controversy in Ferguson remained unresolved. Lingering quietude never quite settled in permanently due to relentless unrest. Just when things seemed peaceful, some external disturbance offered an unwelcome reminder of the malevolent spirit that hovered nearby. The tinderbox in our backyard was one spark away from exploding all over again. The Grand Jury process crawled at a snail's pace and the prospect of a decision hung over us like a pesky swarm of mosquitoes that refused to disperse.

Our blessings surely outweighed our troubles with the two often intertwined. This proved to be the case for Carl Thomas. Sometimes misfortune followed him around like a hungry stray. During his sophomore year, his mother suffered a stroke that largely incapacitated her. Unable to work, she survived on assistance that couldn't cover Carl's tuition. Thankfully, they received some aid from Lutheran North but a shortfall remained. Carl worked 3 to 4 nights a week busing tables at Norwood Hills Country Club to cover the difference. Not one to complain, he kept his nose to the grindstone and never missed school or practice ... and always capped his cheerful demeanor with a smile. Carl excelled in the classroom with a near-perfect GPA of 3.7. No sad sack despite his problems, Carl instead inspired his teammates and coaches. A field general like J-Bay, Carl helped other players remember their assignments on offense and defense. Although greatly gifted, Carl's work ethic outshined all of his other talents.

Carl's positive influence extended to people in all walks of life at LN: students, teachers, administrators and coaches. He helped to instill confidence and trust in everyone. A caring and generous individual, we all rooted for Carl to succeed. It was easy to get behind a guy like Carl, especially for his teammates. Carl's hard work, determination and sunny outlook, despite his personal circumstances, made it easier for everyone else to go the extra mile. Carl's example helped to take our minds off of the depressing situation in Ferguson. The way he overcame his personal challenges helped to cut the seemingly monumental problems facing Ferguson down to size.

Carl served as a one man wrecking crew when it came to obliterating harmful and ugly stereotypes that formed in some folk's minds about the good people of Ferguson. Carl was a case in point regarding God's promises about adversity. God didn't allow more than he could bear. Carl possessed more than his share of difficulties but God also supplied him with an abundance of strength and character; mental, physical and spiritual. Moreover, when all else failed, God provided a means of escape.

One of the crosses we bore as a football team was our lack of sheer numbers. This became more apparent as the season wore on. This problem increased as we entered the home stretch in October. Injuries and inevitable defections stretched our thin squad to the breaking point. Thankfully, we received some relief in the nick of time. Two mid-season transfers met eligibility requirements. Brothers Donald and Josh Harris provided a much needed boost. Although not stars or high impact players, both made meaningful contributions. Young Donnie couldn't claim varsity playing time but, as a lineman, even if somewhat undersized, provided a welcome addition to our practices. He helped to prepare our starters and made us a better team on game day. Josh possessed good size and respectable speed. It took a little time but, once acclimated, he earned a fair amount of playing time on the varsity where he made a positive contribution.

Another set of brothers joined us mid-season. Berrion and Cameron Russell-Clemons had lots of natural talent but, unfortunately, were not eligible to participate in games until 2015. Lots of guys might have opted out until the next season but not Berrion and Cam. They showed maturity and wisdom beyond their years by coming out to practice every day like full-fledged members of the squad. This represented an enormous time commitment as well as a significant investment of hard work for a couple of guys that would never taste glory in 2014.

It paid off handsomely for them and us. The brothers improved their skills and learned our system to be able to hit the ground running in 2015. In Cam and Berrion, the Crusaders gained more than just additional able bodies in practice. Berrion lacked some polish as an underclassman but clearly represented a baller with a bright future. Cam stood out immediately. He played wide receiver and cornerback and shined at both. In practice, Cam pushed our established players to get better. Even our top stars stepped up their games in practice to compete with Cam.

Cam and Berrion provided much more than practice fodder and were quickly adopted into our football family even though they couldn't play on the weekends. They never slacked off or offered excuses because they weren't eligible for games. Cam and Berrion were totally invested in Crusader football. Cam caught the coaches' eyes with his frequent flashes of brilliance. I never expected to see another pair of hands like Brandon Sumrall's but was astounded as Cam routinely made highlight reel, one-handed grabs in practice. He dazzled just as much on defense. As a corner, he delighted in lining up against our top receivers and provided such tight coverage it seemed like their jerseys were sewn together. One day I noticed something that, I joked, revealed the secret to his talent. Cam's thumbs looked about a half inch longer than his other fingers. I ribbed him that he was a freak of nature. "No wonder you've got such great hands … just look at those thumbs! Where do you buy your gloves … are they custom tailored?"

Just as good fortune smiled on us, adversity returned to claim Brandon Sumrall. He suffered a nagging shoulder injury that got progressively worse as the season wore on. He still played but it limited what he could do. Brandon continued to line up at receiver, no matter what, but his shoulder couldn't take the punishment of tackling so we removed him from the defense. In effect, we lost half a man and incurred another major blow to the team. Coach Simmons took it in stride and noted that, when injuries happened, other fellas had to step up. Brandon's bum shoulder affected his play as a receiver but almost imperceptibly due to his grit and determination. He played through the pain and overcame his limitations by taking advantage of his incredible hands. Brandon played so well that it masked the seriousness of his injury. It became fully apparent in the off season when he went under the surgeon's scalpel.

We seemed in limbo after we escaped disaster at Lutheran South. Somehow, we needed to shake off the Burroughs hangover and get our ship back on course. We knew a great game required a great week of practice. Unfortunately, fate threw us a curve at an inopportune time. We faced a short week with the next game against MICDS slated for Thursday night, October 2nd at SLUH's field. Field conditions at MICDS precipitated the mid-week arrangement. SLUH graciously made their stadium available but had their own game on Friday night. It was hard to get the Crusaders fully prepared since we forfeited 2 days of practice. Yet, on a wet night, we appreciated playing on an artificial turf field.

MICDS had a good squad but, on paper, we should have been favored by a fair margin.

However, football is not played on paper and MICDS had other plans for us. Things started out well enough but, as the game went on; they pulled within striking distance and threatened to upset us.

Still stuck in a rut, we struggled to recapture the same efficiency and intensity that served us so well against Burroughs. Doubts arose like the blustery winds that spat rain in our faces. Like the South game, we needed someone to step up and make a play. This time, the source of our inspiration came from perhaps the most unexpected player imaginable, our girl kicker, Karsten. For many weeks, I offered advice to Special K on her kickoff coverage. Normally, she hung way back behind the rest of the kickoff team, ostensibly as our safety valve. In reality, we feared an injury.

Since I also wanted her to avoid embarrassment, I encouraged her to creep up closer to the action. We didn't intend for her to make a tackle but entertained the possibility she might steer the kick returner toward someone else who could make the stop. She understood my rationale. If she stayed 15 yards behind the kickoff team and a kick returner broke free, she'd be all alone and vulnerable to being juked out of her headband, so to speak, by a shifty, speeding runner.

We experimented with this in practice but it never came into play in a game. Against MICDS, Karsten followed instructions well and moved up closer, no more than 5 yards behind the kick coverage. Thankfully, the Rams' kick returners never got far enough to test our theory that her presence might steer them toward another would be tackler. As Murphy's Law dictated, MICDS waited until the game was at a critical juncture to challenge our hypothesis.

We clung to a precipitous 2-point lead as the clock wore down but had to kick off to the Rams one more time. Attuned to stopping their offense from mounting a final scoring drive, we were less concerned about the kickoff. Against all expectations, the Rams' kick returner sliced through our coverage and squirted into the open. It appeared that all was lost. Our girly girl kicker, Karsten, stood alone as the only player between the speeding runner and the end zone. The runner had freed himself from the pack enough that simply steering him toward another tackler wasn't an option. Just as the agonizing reality of defeat set in, something completely amazing happened. Special K cut off the angle like a seasoned veteran and sacrificed herself by flinging her body at the runner. Karsten dropped him like a bag of door knobs!

Our sideline erupted in uproarious cheers. K-Money saved the day! Most importantly, she seemed none the worse for wear. It probably shook her up but, if so, she disguised it well. She seemed to float on air as we swamped her on the sideline. Karsten accomplished much in her one season as a Crusader football player. As if breaking the gender barrier wasn't enough, she set the all-time, single season record of most extra points kicked at 56. Although we preferred to get into the end zone, even on fourth down and long rather than kick a field goal, her 56 points scored wound up being the fourth most points scored by a kicker in a single season at North. In spite of this noteworthy achievement, I believe Special K got more satisfaction out of that tackle than anything else she accomplished as a Crusader.

We dodged another bullet and escaped with a narrow, 37-35 victory and kept our hopes alive. The MICDS game and, in part, Karsten's inspired play, helped us to shake off the post-Burroughs malaise that threatened to derail our 2014 season. We regained our equilibrium just in time to face our neighborhood rival, Trinity, at home on October 11th for homecoming. After close scares from South and MICDS and in remembering last year's debacle where we almost blew such a huge lead against the Titans, our practices were intensely focused. This helped immensely since homecoming week typically destroyed the team's concentration. Coach Simmons chided the boys about being more worried about their outfits and coiffures than the Titans. It made for some good laughs but they got the message. This time around, we left no doubt and put Trinity away in workmanlike fashion, 47-6. The coaching staff had few complaints other than we hated missing the goose egg.

When we heard the news that Burroughs beat, Westminster, we experienced the type of unbridled joy we felt when we topped the Bombers. Westminster beat us, we beat Burroughs and the Bombers beat them. Consequently, we shared the Metro League Conference title in a 3-way tie. Although not an outright title, a share of the crown seemed sweeter considering our pitiful chances after our loss to Westminster. We enjoyed the moment but only briefly. One more game remained in the regular season against our final nonconference foe, St. Mary's. Having captured a conference title, it would have been easy to look past St. Mary's toward districts and the playoffs. However, we kept our heads and secured another solid, if not stellar, victory at 35-6 over the Dragons. The win satisfied the coaches except that, again, we missed out on the goose egg.

Playoff time arrived and this made it easier to forget about Ferguson temporarily, even though we still awaited the Grand Jury decision. The playoffs offered up a whole new season. It provided a new lease on life. This represented do or die time; a win-or-go-home proposition. Unfortunately, two things happened to put a damper on what otherwise would have been a joyous time. First, as the top seed in our district, the schedule slotted us to play Principia, the lowest seed. No matter how hard we tried, no one believed this would be a competitive game. Two months had passed but how could we forget the 72-7 thrashing we administered earlier? Principia dreaded the game more so and elected to forfeit rather than suffer another shellacking. It went into the record books as a 2-0 Crusader victory. The forfeit assured us of moving on to the second round. Beyond that, it meant a 2-week layoff where we might get rusty without actual game competition. From hindsight, we preferred a blowout to no game at all.

Something happened that radically altered our perspective and helped draw a distinction between mere hardships and true adversity. One of our senior stalwarts, happy-go-lucky Nick McGrue, faced a situation that far exceeded anything we encountered on the football field. His older sister, Mia, suffered with illness for many of her 27 years.

Dealing with the serious affliction of a loved one often proved tougher than a personal malady. Nick's cheerful comportment and outstanding performance on the football belied the trying circumstances he faced the entire season. Mia languished with diabetes as she waited to receive kidney and pancreas transplants. Once completed, Mia experienced severe difficulties in her recovery. In and out of the hospital in critical condition for over 2 months, she eventually required hospice care. Mia passed into heavenly glory on October 25th, the day of the Principia forfeit. Nick was like a brother to us so, his loss affected us all.

As it turned out, the break from football proved to be a good thing in that it allowed time for Nick to grieve and afforded his teammates and coaches the opportunity to show our support. Nick exhibited a quiet, stout faith in dealing with the loss of his beloved sister, Mia. Football provided a blessing to him in that it helped Nick to turn his focus from grief. The solace of brotherhood assuaged his pain.

During the 2-week lull, Nick's quiet strength in the face of his tragic loss inspired the team while the dark pall passed over us. Football practice afforded a welcome diversion. It gave us a common goal and purpose. Our next district opponent was Trinity, the team we dispatched handily only 3 weeks before. The coaches fretted over what surely seemed to some as an easy ticket into the next round. It was difficult, at any level of football, to beat the same team twice within a season. Knowing our tendencies allowed for strategic adjustments by Trinity. It also provided the revenge factor. We knew from 2013 that anything could happen when it came to a matchup between North and Trinity.

The coaches pondered the effect of the 2-week layoff. Would our guys be rusty or complacent, or take Trinity for granted? Nick's loss weighed on us too. Could we take football seriously after the cold reality of death visited one of our young brothers? As if we didn't have enough on our minds, the threat of violence reared its ugly head again. Word leaked out that the Grand Jury decision might be forthcoming. Here's what Mr. Brackman had to say in his communication memo of October 30th, 2014:

"There will likely be an announcement of the Grand Jury's findings in the Michael Brown case within the near future. We don't know whether this will take place within the next days or weeks but it is apparent that the time will come soon. Regardless of their decision, we must recognize that the situation may become volatile once again."

We knew it had to happen sometime. Mr. Brackman offered some practical safety tips but still it unnerved us. The warning came at a terrible time for the football team. We didn't need another diversion and a major one at that. Consequently, uncertainty followed us into the next round. Could we ignore the troubling distraction and avoid the mistakes of the past? We learned a hard lesson against Westminster and, since then, experienced two close calls against South and MICDS when we lost focus. We felt we were a different team now that God had strengthened us through our trials. As for the Ferguson situation, our God-given faith proved sufficient. We were golden against the Titans and finally secured the long sought after but elusive goose egg in a convincing 35-0 victory.

As it turned out, the Grand Jury speculation proved to be a false alarm. It provided an ominous reminder and served to raise fresh doubt and fears in the surrounding community. It also led to more frustration for protestors and others who couldn't fathom why the justice system moved so painfully slow. As a football team, we were concerned with more pressing matters.

Next up, we faced the kind of team that gave us fits in the past. We had a tougher time adjusting to farm boys who played simple, hard-nosed, downhill football. Hermann wasn't in a league with the likes of Lamar but had a similar, straightforward style that didn't involve a lot of guesswork. They lined up and came right at opponents with a preference for pounding the ball. We prepared for a battle in the trenches... It produced another methodical, convincing win, 48-12.

We stood at another crossroads. From the onset, we set lofty goals. We planned to run the table in the regular season, win the conference crown, claim a district championship and secure a state title. The latter meant exorcising our demons. We needed to erase the painful memory of our embarrassing loss to Lamar that ended our 2013 season. It all seemed lost when an unfortunate bounce produced a loss to Westminster 3 games into the season. Yet, we were only a step away from fulfilling our dreams. We shared the conference crown, ran the table after Westminster and won the district title for the second year in a row. At times in 2014, we faced what seemed like an avalanche of adversity, both individually and collectively. No other team lived within the shadow of imminent danger like we did as a result of the so called Ferguson-effect. Yet somehow, God pulled us through and we were poised to reach the pinnacle.

Chapter 14: From Orbit to Crash Landing

Flying high among only 8 teams left in the hunt, we felt fortunate to be only 3 wins away from the a Class 2 state title. We stood tall after facing so many obstacles. Now we encountered the challenge of being road warriors. Slated to face Palmyra on Saturday, November 15[th,] this meant an early start and a 2-hour bus ride to the outskirts of Hannibal, MO. The overcast sky, bitter chill and dreary weather kept us in a serious, even somber mood on the ride up to Palmyra. This seemed like a good sign to the coaches but it was hard to predict how the team's mood might translate into performance on the field.

The Panthers, another bunch of tough farm boys, seemed, on film, a notch above Hermann and possessed the grit and determination embodied in their nose guard/middle linebacker, Matt Frankenbach. Number 75 stood about 6' 3" and weighed 250 pounds but we were most impressed by his intensity. On HUDL, he seemed to have a great motor and caused a lot of problems for opposing offenses. He roamed everywhere, seemingly always in the right place at the right time. From our perspective, this provided an opportunity for our massive offensive line to exert their will. We hoped we could turn this game into a track meet and utilize our superior team speed. This shaped up to be a classic matchup between their raw power and our speed. We figured we held the edge since we had plenty of strength and power to go along with our thoroughbred speedsters.

The loss of David Still worked to our serious disadvantage. Sidelined by a concussion, this eliminated half of our one-two punch out of the backfield. He felt he could play but it was out of the question, as a matter of health and safety. We needed to get past Palmyra without him and give his recovery another week. David's absence shackled us in the worst way since we needed his hard-nosed, downhill running style to negate some of their strength along the defensive front. However, we still possessed an ace in the hole. Carl Thomas, just as tough as David, brought other things to the mix: lateral skills, elusiveness and an uncanny ability to break free for long gallops. Eager anticipation flitted in our stomachs and electricity filled the air as we waited for the first whistle.

It became apparent almost immediately that we needed to toss out everything we anticipated on paper. A tight, defensive struggle ensued as Palmyra reduced our high flying, thrill-a-minute offense to pedestrian standards We could not get untracked as Frankenbach played like a man possessed and wreaked havoc along the defensive front. He lived in our backfield and it also seemed he had invaded the heads of our offensive lineman. He was Kryptonite to our supermen. We couldn't run the ball so we tried to air it out. Unfortunately, Frankenbach's relentless pursuit forced J-Bay to scramble for his life. Extremely frustrated as coaches, we simply couldn't execute. Our normally well-oiled machine coughed and sputtered as if someone replaced our rocket fuel with molasses.

Thankfully, our defense kept pace with the Panthers except for the one early touchdown we allowed. We looked for a morale boost by surviving the half tied or down only 7-0. However, misfortune struck just before the break. Their quarterback lofted a mid-range pass near where one of our linebackers, Josh Harris, dropped back into coverage. Well-positioned against the opposing receiver, Josh jumped up for an interception that could have been returned for a Crusader touchdown. He came up a half inch short and the ball glanced off his fingertips. Incredibly, the tipped pass fluttered deeper downfield into the unsuspecting hands of another Panther receiver. It kept their drive alive and they scored a touchdown to take a 14-0 lead.

Fickle fate frowned on us that day. We learned later that one of Josh's arms was a little shorter than the other; the outstretched limb that strained to haul in the interception. We remained resolute in spite of a mood in the locker room that resembled the gloomy weather. Not ones to give up without a fight, our thoughts turned to games like South and MICDS where perseverance and faith paid off.

We struggled to maintain a positive mindset as the second half got underway. Our passing game remained moribund but we didn't concede anything. The Crusaders took Coach Simmons at his word and clawed and scratched for every inch. Although we preferred a wide open game, we realized that sometimes even great teams needed to adapt to overcome such hurdles. Finally, our determination and collective effort paid off. We maintained a long drive that culminated in the end zone and closed the gap to a single touchdown. Then disaster of the worst kind struck when we lost our heart and soul as Carl Thomas suffered a crippling knee injury. It devastated our team since Carl was our inspirational leader. He, more than anyone else on the team, could face any adversity and prevail. Without him, the hill we tried to climb became Mt. Everest.

Our last option, Martize Jenkins, was a talented, gutsy player but still just a pint-sized freshman. With Martize not built to blast through the meat grinder in the trenches, everything fell on the shoulders of our field general, Justin Baker. We had to get it done through the air. Unfortunately, J-Bay experienced an off day. He lacked his normal accuracy and the loss of his brother-in-arms, Carl Thomas, ravaged his spirit. All the while he faced ferocious harassment from Matt Frankenbach and company who continued to maraud through our backfield at will. It truly looked hopeless. Every drive stalled like an old car with a clogged carburetor as the clock wound down. Most other teams might have thrown in the towel but not Justin Baker and the Crusaders who remained determined to fight with everything left in their arsenal until the last bell.

Less than 2 minutes remained and it seemed impossible we could post the tying score. The line of scrimmage appeared much too far away from pay dirt. Any yards gained came slowly and methodically and too few ticks remained on the clock. Undaunted, J-Bay rallied his offense for one last, gallant effort. The line fought valiantly and Justin scrambled away from onrushing linemen as if he had channeled Fran Tarkington. Despite the wet, muddy conditions, Justin managed to put just enough zip on the ball. Our receivers willed their way to get open and Brandon Sumrall flashed his magic hands again. Somehow, against incredible odds, we marched the length of the field and had the ball on the Panthers' 5 yard line with just 5 seconds left. Down to our last hurrah, could the Crusaders pull a rabbit out of the hat and send the game into overtime? Justin dodged a furious rush and launched the ball toward the corner of the end zone as the clock ran out. It floated a bit high, just beyond a leaping Brandon's outstretched arms, and sailed out of the back of the end zone. The wild cheers that emanated from the Panthers and their jubilant fans drowned out our grief and anguish.

We were numb as we packed up our equipment, piled onto the bus and headed back for the somber ride home that seemed like 10 hours rather than 2. How did this happen to the team of destiny? We came so close only to fall shy once again! Despite all of our talent, fickle fate denied us our dream. As planned for November, we headed east on I-70 toward the Dome but, in despair, exited well short of our intended destination onto Lucas & Hunt. Worse, our friend and brother, Carl Thomas, was felled by a nasty knee injury. What did this portend for his previously bright future? Had it squashed his hopes for a football scholarship and good education?

What about the other seniors? For 20 on our squad, this represented their last high school game. For many, never to suit up again, organized football was finished. Our hearts lamented as the finality of it sunk in. The coaching staff couldn't look ahead to next year, not yet. Down in the dumps, we only pondered what could have been.

I wondered if it was the end of the line for me too. With my bum shoulder as sore as ever, old age seemed to catch up with me as I fast approached 60. I still cherished the bond of brotherhood shared with my fellow coaches but many of the players I loved like extended family faced graduation. This introspection added to my melancholy so, I looked to God's wisdom as I mulled over our depressing circumstances. Then I remembered that our common faith in Jesus Christ provided the bond that held us together through all the ups and downs, including Carl's debilitating injury and Nick's loss of his sister. With that in mind and in having a captive audience, I did what seemed natural. A devotion with my 2014 Crusader family seemed in order since it might be our last chance together. The gospel of Jesus Christ supplied the sure remedy for all of our troubles. With that, we ended on a glorious high note.

The season ended abruptly but football continued as a year-round endeavor. While many of our players moved onto basketball, unfinished football business remained. This year proved different in that Dan Wenger exchanged his

Assistant Principal's hat for a coach's cap. Dan tapped into his wrestling roots to help launch the Crusader's inaugural grappling squad. Some of our guys like Robert Brown and David Knox swapped their pads and helmets for togs and gave it a go. As football coaches, we liked the idea. Wrestling offered another way to keep up with conditioning in the offseason. Unlike 2013, this offseason required much more attention to college recruiting. With 20 seniors and such a wealth of talent, we had quite a few prospects. Most didn't anticipate Division 1 offers but that mattered little. Division 2 also offered the opportunity to use football as a means of securing a good education.

Carl Thomas represented our best shot at a Division 1 scholarship, at least until he suffered torn ligaments in his knee. It was cruelly ironic that this happened in his last high school game. Carl persevered so well through an incredible string of bad luck but couldn't catch a break. As if the potentially career-ending injury wasn't enough, the kitchen caught fire at Carl's house the day after the Palmyra game. It left their home, a rental unit, unlivable. Carl and his mother moved in with his grandmother. This made Carl's already shaky financial situation even more tenuous. Due to poor health care coverage, Carl waited almost a month for a MRI and proper diagnosis on the day before

Christmas break. His knee required extensive repairs yet, somehow, Carl returned to school only 2 days after the surgery and never missed a single assignment. He maintained his stellar performance in the classroom despite the difficulties of living in the cramped confines of his grandmother's house for 4 months and suffering through the rigors of rehabilitation.

Just as we seemed to turn the corner, more adversity awaited Carl and his fellow schoolmates at North. Thanks to Mike Williams and our other friends on the police force, Mr. Brackman and his Crisis Team stayed abreast of developments in the Michael Brown case. While our football team had been consumed with the upcoming Palmyra game, Mr. Brackman issued this communication on November 10th, 2014:

"Dear Crusader students and families,

As an update to the email sent last week regarding the Grand Jury's findings in the Michael Brown case, we learned last Friday that there will not be an announcement prior to November 15th. This has also been verified in the local news. It is still unclear whether an announcement will be made soon after the 15th or not.

The Crisis Team continues to meet and make plans for potential cancellations, early dismissals, or other scenarios which may result. If possible, we will continue to have school. Of course, we will always act in the best interest of everyone's safety. We feel that maintaining a sense of what's normal is also important.

Because what will transpire is simply unknown, we expect that students will take all of their class materials with them each evening following November 14th, just in case there is an announcement and activities prohibit us from being in school. If this happens, teachers will be communicating with students via their school email accounts and relevant coursework and/or assignments will be forthcoming as well. All students will be fully responsible for any class activities and/or assignments that are shared in this way.

Of course, we are praying that things do not develop as many have warned. I cannot express to you strongly enough how peaceful and wonderful our students have been throughout this entire chain of events. God is orchestrating awesome things each and every day within the walls of Lutheran North and now, more than ever, it is clear how important our diverse educational community of Christians is!"

Being put on high alert in this fashion proved upsetting for parents, students and everyone involved. The long saga that played out ominously on our door step came to a head and not a pretty one. Many in the media, law enforcement and government warned that the situation posed greater potential for violence than the bedlam we witnessed in the first days after the shooting. I believe most people shared a strong inkling of the decision we faced. Mike Williams knew from day one that the hands up, don't shoot narrative was a false one. Now, most informed people shared this awareness. An indictment seemed unlikely. What caused the long delay? Had officials waited for the right time to deliver the bad news? Could the Thanksgiving holiday quell some of the inevitable backlash?

The timing appeared to be more than coincidental to me. The Grand Jury's decision came down on Monday. This allowed 3 days for any unrest to boil over before it hopefully dissipated by Thursday, November 27th, Thanksgiving Day. Mr. Brackman and his Crisis Team faced a critical decision. They avoided shutting down the school for 4 months, except for the 3 days in August it took to repair the water main break. Confronted with grave uncertainty, Mr. Brackman issued this announcement on November 24th:

"In light of the Grand Jury decision, we have cancelled all activities for this evening. We request that all students be picked up as soon as possible and not later than 5:00 p. m. We are praying for a peaceful resolution to the situation. God Bless."

Later the same day, LN delivered this recorded phone message to everyone:

"Dear Crusader families,

This is Mr. Brackman calling from Lutheran North. In light of tonight's Grand Jury announcement and the unpredictable nature of upcoming events, we will not have a regular school day tomorrow. Instead, we WILL have an e-learning day. This means students will be learning from home.

Last Friday, instructions were sent about how this type of virtual learning school day will work. I'm sure that there will be some questions but we will work our way through them. I ask that you do your best to carry on even in this very difficult time. More information will be forthcoming from your teachers and administrators. Be sure to check your school email account often and follow the instructions included.

I am very saddened by these events but know that our God is more powerful than anything the devil throws at us. Remember the words of Jesus from John Chapter 14, 'Peace I leave with you; my peace I give to you. Not as the world gives do I give to you. Let not your hearts be troubled, neither let them be afraid.'

God bless you all and good night."

These words of wisdom, so foreign to most public school settings, reflected more than convenient platitudes. Everyone knew these heartfelt truths came from a faithful man who remained consistent throughout the long, trying ordeal. After so many weeks of normalcy, Lutheran North finally succumbed to practicality. Shutting down school for a single day set a new, unwelcome precedent.

Things looked bleak. Our Crusader football team, a source of pride and inspiration, plummeted from our lofty orbit the week before. Now, it seemed, the whole school suffered a crash landing of a different sort. Nevertheless, adversity proved to be a blessing once again. Mr. Brackman demonstrated great leadership and refused to let the cancellation impede the learning process. Most importantly, he pointed everyone to the one, sure thing that kept our Crusader vessel from crashing onto the rocks in the surrounding, storm-tossed seas. Jesus Christ remained our anchor and His word was our rudder.

Chapter 15: Aftermath

Pandemonium ensued after the Grand Jury refused to indict Darren Wilson and deemed the shooting of Michael Brown as justifiable self-defense. The volcanic unrest that erupted immediately thereafter eased somewhat over Thanksgiving but, to the disappointment of many, regained momentum after the holiday. The intensity eventually abated but the never-ending protests maintained a life of their own. Ferguson achieved celebrity status as the epicenter for the Black Lives Matter movement. Although largely debunked, the hands up, don't shoot narrative remained a rallying cry. It became a national phenomenon. Frankly, many people in and around Ferguson and the St. Louis area grew tired of the situation. For all intents and purposes, it was settled except for one last hope for the unrequited avengers among us. Would the Federal investigation yield different results?

At Lutheran North, we resumed a more normal routine even though we still faced challenges. Our campus remained largely an idyllic sanctuary amidst the turmoil. However, we couldn't escape our humanity, warts and all. Although we shared a common faith and outlook on life, we saw the events of Ferguson from a variety of perspectives. The football team's unity represented an anomaly generated by the singular purpose that dominated our outlook. In other, less regimented walks of life, our students held to a wide variety of opinions across a myriad of subjects. At their age, emotions often swayed viewpoints that were expressed with a lot of passion. It didn't take much for honest debate to devolve into heated words or even open conflict. This occasionally required administrators and teachers to serve as referees.

As pressures mounted, some in North's student body reached a tipping point. For the most part we enjoyed incredible peace and normalcy, given everything that transpired nearby, but time took its toll. Our students lived with the Ferguson-Effect for 4 long months. Social media, a blessing and a curse, became an outlet for some kids' frustrations and this provided administrators and teachers with a uniquely modern challenge. It required them to monitor a virtual world beyond the buildings and campus. While things appeared calm in the classroom, tensions sometimes boiled over in chatrooms. Electronic media emboldened people to express things they would never say face-to-face in polite conversation. I've experienced this sad phenomenon in email wars and road rage incidents.

Although amazingly united and incredibly disciplined throughout the Ferguson ordeal, ongoing pressure created a few fissures amongst the student body. According to Mr. Brackman but without naming any names, one illustrative, social media flare up occurred during the Thanksgiving break. It involved a small but diverse group of students: one black, one white and the third was bi-racial. Several times, the media interviewed the black student who took an active role in the protests. A nice kid from a good family, he embraced the notion that Ferguson represented a more widespread problem in our society between the police and minority communities. Normally outspoken, something he tweeted or posted on Facebook rubbed someone the wrong way and resulted in a cyber scrum. They exchanged some harsh words and it threatened to turn into ugly rather than civil discourse.

Mr. Brackman got wind of the trouble and took immediate steps to defuse the situation. He never tried to clamp down on open dialogue but simply steered people to share their differences in a more constructive fashion. This confrontation, among other concerns, prompted this chapel announcement on December 1st, the first day after returning from the Thanksgiving break. These are the notes that Mr. Brackman used to guide his thoughts and comments:

"We have all lived through some wild events over the past week. Like you, I have experienced a wide variety of emotions. We understand … you may be: tired, scared, offended, frustrated, sympathetic, confused, feel that justice has been served, that there is no justice in this and want your voice to be heard. All of these emotions are normal and healthy and you are entitled to them. As I said back in August, you are entitled to your opinions but so is the person next to you.

I have learned how life works HERE at LN! I grew up in a white, vanilla world. I have gained so much from our school. **This place is different!** We have unity because of our **relationships** … with Christ and each other.

We care about all of you! We've gotten to know each other. We still have disagreements.

We need to use our social media presence to honor LN both on and off campus."

Mr. Brackman's kind, caring and Christ-centered outlook provided a practical and soothing remedy for what ailed the Crusaders. This approach helped to reinforce the fabric of North's close knit community and prevented excesses that might have otherwise torn us apart.

Mr. Wenger applied this same approach soon thereafter when another potential disruption threatened to cause divisions among us. The same student who participated regularly in the protests tried to organize a walkout to demonstrate our solidarity with other schools in the area that staged simultaneous events on December 1st. LN empathized with the good folks of Ferguson and often tried to show our support in a number of tangible ways. While the proposed walkout reflected good intentions and seemed consistent with our general approach, it entailed some troubling drawbacks.

Mr. Wenger tackled this conundrum by comparing the walkout to another, more typical event where North hosted a fund raiser with the help of the Ferguson Burger Bar. The proprietors, Charles and Kizzie Davis, graduated from Lutheran North and served as benefactors to others in the area. In a fun, collaborative effort, our students and the Davises donated the proceeds from their burger sales to Ferguson. This helped business people harmed by the destruction and looting. A private affair without links to other organizations or causes, it didn't interfere with North's normal routine or other priorities.

Mr. Wenger took this into account in seeking a fair solution. The administration didn't have a problem with showing North's compassion for those who felt that justice hadn't been fully served. They never wavered from the belief that everyone is entitled to their opinion. Even if they personally disagreed with someone's position, they tried to protect their right to espouse it openly. However, a walkout ran counter to a couple of core principles. The first required us to honor the Lord in all things and the second assigned a top priority to promoting learning. Dan Wenger worked out a healthy compromise with the student sponsor.

North demonstrated understanding and sympathy without compromising its principles. Instead of a walkout, Lutheran North observed a moment of silence on December 1st followed by a schoolwide prayer. This kind of leadership and good, thoughtful conduct among the students carried the day on December 1st and forward. Normalcy and faithfulness prevailed despite the continued unrest and social turmoil in nearby Ferguson and elsewhere.

Although it had nothing to do with social upheaval, the Crusader football team faced tumultuous times in in the offseason. We faced the monumental task of replacing the vast majority of our starters. When we lost the bulk of our starters to graduation it required more than just having a lot of young guys step up. We also needed to add quite a few new players to the mix. At least we enjoyed the benefit of a strong, seasoned staff to guide us through the process. Although we counted on this, the winds of change blew us out of our comfort zone. The most significant turn of events involved our head coach, Brian Simmons. He supplied the glue that held it all together. Fortunately for him and not so fortuitously for us, Coach Simmons received a new calling. His alma mater, Bishop Dubourg High School, called him home to be their Head Football Coach and Dean of Students.

This fantastic opportunity presented Coach Simmons with an agonizing dilemma. Coach loved Lutheran North and genuinely cared about our players, his kids. He sincerely cherished the bond we coaches shared as brothers. In some ways, as a football coach, he preferred to stay at his new home, Lutheran North, rather than return to his alma mater. However, this offered a chance to take an important step forward in his career. As much as I wanted him to stay at Lutheran North, I couldn't argue against the move. This represented something new, a chance to use his talent and skills to help kids in a completely different way as an administrator. I felt it could lead to even greater responsibility someday, perhaps as a superintendent.

Faced with a difficult decision, Coach Simmons did the right thing and made the hard choice. We were greatly saddened but, more so, joyful over his good fortune and the blessings he would surely impart to others. As a football team, it meant more uncertainty for us. It placed the heaviest burden on our young AD, Jon Mueller. Faced with a huge void, he started a search for the next head coach and anticipated other openings from the ripple effects of Coach Simmons' departure. I took it as a sign that maybe the time was right for me to make a clean break. It made sense with Coach Simmons gone, a shake-up in his staff likely and many of our players moving on. I contemplated hanging up my cleats and turning my focus back to writing, consulting, grandkids and the like.

Jon Mueller, wise beyond his years and endowed with a strong faith, forged ahead in the face of daunting responsibilities. His duties as Athletic Director spanned all sports and the entire school. Plus, he coached football and baseball. At least with an established coach like Brian Simmons in the fold, he never worried about the stability of the football program. Now, with all of his priorities shuffled, the coaching search occupied much of his time. Pressure mounted as the demands on his time seemed to reach the limit. Then, at seemingly the worst possible time, another more foreboding development put Jon's strength and faith to the test in a way that made his other mounting, day-to-day challenges pale in comparison.

Jon and his wife Jamie were blessed with a 3-year-old son, Jared, and felt it was time to expand their family. It thrilled them when Jamie became pregnant in February, 2015.Their joy abruptly turned to sorrow on March 3rd. Jamie was only 5 weeks along when she miscarried.

To the rest of us, it appeared they took this terrible setback in stride. They wore brave faces but such a tragedy must have weighed on their souls. They demonstrated rock solid faith and didn't blame God or turn away from His word. To their credit, Jon and Jamie demonstrated faith in action by quickly deciding to try again to bless Jared with a brother or sister. Their willingness to trust in the Lord and forge ahead set a great example for all of us.

Our respite was short due to the ever present Ferguson-effect. Worldly peace seemed so elusive. However, we understood the true nature of peace. Christ Jesus addressed the topic of temporal peace this way in Matthew 10:34-36, "Think not that I am come to send peace on earth: I came not to send peace, but a sword. For I am come to set a man at variance against his father, and the daughter against her mother, and the daughter in law against her mother in law. And a man's foes shall be they of his own household." Jesus pointed to the simple truth in this passage. Even close family members got caught up in rancorous disputes when it came to His gospel message. If spiritual matters led to strife and divisions, we couldn't expect anything different when it came to worldly matters like race relations.

When Christ said that He came to bring a sword, He referred to a spiritual weapon, His holy word (Ephesians 6:17) that could divide asunder soul and spirit and discerned the thoughts and intents of the heart (Hebrews 4:12). When Jesus spoke of true peace, He referred to the kind of true, lasting peace that Mr. Brackman cited in John 14:27, "Peace I leave with you, my peace I give unto you: not as the world giveth, give I unto you. Let not your heart be troubled, neither let it be afraid." Only believers could experience this kind of true peace. The truth of God's word afforded the peace that passed all human understanding, even in the midst of adversity, danger, hardship and tragedy. This is how Jesus put it in John 16:33, "These things I have spoken unto you, that in me ye might have peace. In the world ye shall have tribulation: but be of good cheer; I have overcome the world."

It wasn't long before more worldly tribulation ensued in Ferguson and beyond. On March 4th,

2015, the Justice Department released the results of the Federal investigation. Like the Grand Jury, they cleared Darren Wilson of any civil rights violations and deemed the hands up, don't shoot narrative inaccurate. They recommended corrective actions for the Ferguson Police Department and this offered some appeasement for those still seeking justice. Unfortunately, the findings of President Obama's Justice Department didn't lead to reconciliation or a resolution. Some of the local protesters and others within the national movement ignored the facts and continued to promulgate the false, hands up, don't shoot narrative.

One month later, on April 12th, Freddie Gray, Jr. died from a spinal cord injury suffered during transport in a Baltimore police van. Never mind that the circumstances were unique. This immediately became another dot to be connected along with Trayvon Martin, Eric Garner and Michael Brown. Trayvon Martin represented a case of self-defense involving a citizen rather than a police officer. Eric Garner appeared to be a case of excessive police force. The Michael Brown case involved self-defense by a police officer who faced a life-threatening attacker according to credible eye witnesses. The facts were immaterial though. To folks in the movement, this was just another case of systematic, institutionalized police abuse of a minority.

Freddie Gray carried a long rap sheet and, according to some reports, tried to self-inflict an injury. This case encompassed another oddity in that it involved 6 police officers, some male, some female, 3 white and 3 black. There were good reasons to wait for an investigation to sort out the facts. None of that mattered. On April 25, 2015, pandemonium ensued as protests in Baltimore turned violent and destructive. The images on television, eerily similar to what we witnessed in Ferguson, appeared even more intense and widespread.

It saddened many to see a major American city like Baltimore engulfed in sheer, wanton anarchy. The battle cry included the now familiar mantra of hands up, don't shoot. The phrase, Black Lives Matter, also appeared front and center. This proved divisive at a time when we sorely needed healing. In a sense, this racially charged slogan wasn't racist. To some, it offered an honest appeal to recognize the plight of inner city blacks who felt unfairly targeted by police through racial profiling and excessive force and violence. To others, it represented a racially divisive epitaph that unnecessarily poured salt in our nation's wounds and offended white people otherwise sympathetic to the cause.

The authorities in Baltimore didn't help matters. Instead, they fanned the flames of racial animus when the State's Attorney, Marilyn Mosby, eschewed blind justice and made public statements that appeared to show sympathy for the protesters' cause. Based on information released through the media, it seemed that some of the officers might be charged with negligence. Nothing in the public realm appeared to point to willful bodily harm. Nevertheless, Ms. Mosby filed charges against all 6 officers including 2nd degree, depraved-heart murder. It seemed excessive and politically motivated. This stirred up a greater racial divide in the country and changed the outlook of police everywhere. Many felt they were unfairly accused and civilian authorities didn't have their backs. Many openly questioned the wisdom of risking their lives and careers in the line of duty. Ugly signs cropped up in law enforcement around the nation. Cops became purposefully reactive rather than proactive and the public suffered for it.

This made me think of my friend and fellow coach, Detective Mike Williams. I remembered the frustration in his voice when he recounted how the Michael Brown incident raised tension between Mike and some of his relatives. In regard to the hands up, don't shoot narrative he exclaimed to them, "You guys are getting fooled!" When he heard the claims that St. Louis County Prosecutor Bob McCullough was in the tank for Darren Wilson, he explained, "Bob McCullough will not make this decision. It will be the Grand Jury." When some of his relatives and friends argued that Mr. McCullough should be removed as the Prosecutor, Mike said "Fine ... go ahead and remove him but who will replace him? I'm here to tell you that nobody wants to take this case. It's a no-win situation." Mike told me point blank that the police reluctance that led to skyrocketing homicide rates was real. He asked rhetorically, "Is it worth getting shot?" He put it bluntly, "Don't get involved unless you're fired upon. I'd rather be judged by 12 than carried out by 6."

Nothing good came out of the Freddie Gray, Jr. case in Baltimore. Racial tensions grew. Extreme elements in society led a backlash against police. The movement resulted in a spate of police killings, some of which resembled outright assassinations. The police were left to second guess their actions rather than putting the safety and security of the public first. Politicians left business owners in effected areas to fend for themselves. Our country seemed to be coming apart at the seams. In a twisted sense, one fortuitous thing came out of the

Baltimore strife. If misery loved company, we had plenty to go around. In a selfish way, Baltimore helped Ferguson and the St. Louis area. It took us out of the spotlight and diverted the media's pedantic attention to Baltimore.

Race relations in America crumbled around us as the end of the 2014-2015 schoolyear approached. The nation's greater woes put things in perspective and made some of our personal problems seem small in comparison. We faced plenty of difficulties, some quite serious, with a good portion stemming from the movement launched in nearby Ferguson. However, at Lutheran North, we still felt incredibly fortunate as we counted our blessings. Our spiritual state of affairs trumped anything the world threw at us. We owed our thanks to God for this miracle. The peace we enjoyed in the midst of chaos existed by the grace, power, mercy and love of God in Christ.

As for football, the Crusaders still suffered in disarray. We existed as just a team rather than a program and longed for continuity. Without a head coach at the helm and half of our players departing, our legacy seemed hopelessly lost. I regretted abandoning the Crusaders during such upheaval but, for me, it was time to move on.

EPILOGUE
2015 – The Legacy Continues

I prepared to ride off into the sunset and start my next book project. Our football legacy could have simply been this: we remained friends and brothers after going our separate ways. I stayed in regular contact with my coaching buddies like Brian Simmons, Jon Mueller and Kelvin Austin. But our relationships changed since we didn't rub elbows in daily practices or go to battle together on weekends. I heard from some of the players occasionally but they too moved on with their lives as many prepared for college. I was blessed with 3 more grandkids, Steven III, whom I called Threevie, and a pair of twins I labeled the Ws, Will and Wyatt, which brought the total to 7. I kept busy writing, chasing the kiddos or following other pursuits. However, the story didn't end there for me.

Some vexing questions lingered. Were 2013 and 2014 magical slices of time never to be duplicated again? What if Lutheran North succumbed to the Ferguson- Effect? I feared the loss of our miraculous peace to the influence of America's fractured, coarsened society. My hope rested in the many wonderful students, parents, administrators, teachers and coaches with which God had blessed Lutheran North. But names and faces changed with the times and created a threat to the continuity of our school's legacy. For me, football provided an idyllic island within North's paradise world. How could that good fortune continue without Coach Simmons and his merry band? If things changed, how would I know? As an outsider, I forfeited my bird's eye view. Left in the dark, I simply hoped and prayed.

My retirement from Crusader football was short lived though. When I explained to Jon Mueller that I was too old for such a young man's game, he graciously said I was welcome to help out part-time if the spirit moved me. Jon suggested that I could come to practice occasionally and join the Crusaders on the sidelines during games. At first, I just took this as a nice gesture on his part. Then it bored into my head. Curiosity gripped me regarding what lay ahead: the new head coach, staff changes and new players. How would the Crusaders fare under such trying circumstances? What did this mean for some of the returning players? I longed to see Cam realize his star potential. I hoped to see a turnaround by one of my favs, temperamental Cortez Simmons. Did we have a quarterback? I wanted to track the progress of Brandon Sumrall's recovery from shoulder surgery. How good could Jordan Sommerville be with the experience he'd gained plus another year under his belt?

Once I delved into our 2015 prospects, I couldn't turn back. What kind of senior campaigns would our big guys, Robert Brown and David Knox, enjoy? I wanted to see Devin Hart plug one of the big holes left by our departing seniors and watch Malik Mingo hit the big time. Who could run the ball besides the Tezes, Martize and Cortez? I anxiously awaited Dulani's return for his senior year, hopefully tougher and stronger, and anticipated J-Rob taking a lead role. How would the young guys like Berrion, Keyshaun, Ryan Smith and John Smith fare and who would fill all the other gaps? And, who in the world would replace Kicker Karsten? The more I pondered, the more the coaching juices flowed. Could I really make a clean break and put it behind me? The thought gripped me; *maybe Jon's suggestion was more than just a polite sendoff.*

A part-time gig seemed to present the best of all worlds. I could get my coaching fix, stay close to the kids and still have time for my other interests. As the weeks passed, with my curiosity running rampant, this notion grew on me. I wanted to at least give it a try. I needed to see if Jon could keep the ball rolling and build on what Coach Simmons had established. Filling the void at the top proved to be the most difficult and time consuming task. Coach Mueller finally passed along the news that he hired Carl Reed, Jr. to succeed Coach Simmons. He possessed a strong resume and came from a big, familiar program: Hazelwood West. It inured my sensibilities further when Coach Mueller advised that Carl was a fellow Hawk from my alma mater, Hazelwood Central.

This cast Coach Reed in a favorable light, that is, until I met him. An imposing figure as an ex-lineman, Carl Reed's personality resembled a steamroller that might flatten anything in its path. His thick, dark-rimmed glasses and stoic countenance gave him the look of an evil genius. I'm sorry to say, I didn't like him from the get go. Coach Reed didn't strike me as approachable. Was it me or did he dislike and distrust humanity in general? He ran his practices much differently than Coach Simmons. He seemed dictatorial and didn't delegate like Coach Simmons. He lacked Brian's patience and easy going manner. His style seemed much more autocratic and he struck me as some sort of a control freak. Worst of all, his coaching philosophy was anathema to me. Extremely conservative, he promised to rely almost exclusively on the running game. I shuddered at the thought of our high flying offense being dismantled by Coach Reed.

I thought, *maybe this new gig wasn't such a good idea*. He didn't give me a warm, fuzzy feeling. At times, I felt like an interloper rather than part of his crew which was reshaped through significant turnover. In addition to my change in status and Coach Simmons' departure, LN replaced 3 other coaches: Matt Hieke, Josh Cody and Kelvin Austin. Coaches Mueller, Fehrs, Lorenz and Williams remained in the fold but our original group was reduced to only half of what we used to be.

A head coach is best judged by the people surrounding him. Given my negative vibes about Coach Reed, I was predisposed to writing off his new coaches too. However, as I got to know them, I couldn't help but like them. Although quite young, Micah Pomerenke sure knew his football. He seemed like a worthy replacement for Matt Hieke in developing our offensive line. Austin Davis, another young guy and soft spoken to the point of being shy, possessed a good football mind. Both guys played in college and demonstrated a knack for getting through to the young guys. Since Micah graduated from Concordia, Seward, NE, I teased Coach Mueller that the Nebraska connection was getting out of hand since Jon, Troy Fehrs and Mike Lorenz all came from that same pipeline.

Jamison Palmer, another Hawk, was an upper classman at Hazelwood Central when Coach Reed played there. Along with Cortland Johnson, Jamison starred on the Hawks' 1996 state championship team when young Carl still rode the pine mostly. Coach Palmer, the epitome of cool, had the right stuff to guide our running backs since he never got rattled under pressure. Hard to get to know at first, Jarrod Powell turned out to be one of the most likeable fellows on the staff. Perfectly suited to coach the D-line Jarrod still retained a defensive lineman's mentality. He fired guys up with his unbridled, contagious enthusiasm. I related well to Jarod since he loved to win and couldn't stomach losing.

I jumped on Coach John Randle's bandwagon right away. He owned a great resume, having played and served as a graduate assistant at Arkansas-Pine Bluff. He also acquired some head coaching experience at Soldan High School. His unfettered exuberance for the game of football impressed me the most. John served as our Defensive Coordinator but provided much more. Like Coach Cody before him, he became our cheerleader in chief. No one else fired up the troops like Coach Randle. When Coach Cody left, I thought, *we'll never replace him. We just lost our heart and soul.* In Coach Randle, we had our mojo back and Coach Powell's spirit added to this blessing. It delighted me to find that the new coaches were faithful Christian men. The bond of brotherhood remained as strong as ever.

I wondered whether I might be wrong about Coach Reed. How could a guy with such a great staff be so bad? I learned that Coach Simmons and Coach Reed were tight. I knew Coach Simmons to be a great judge of character so my mind opened up a bit. This forced me to look in the mirror. It also, thankfully, convinced me not to pull the plug on my experiment as a part-time coach. Over time, I found out that I had rushed to judgment. Shamefully, I admitted to myself that I hadn't practiced what I'd preached. I judged the book by the cover. The more I got to know Coach Reed on a personal level, the more I liked and respected him. I even admired him.

Eventually, it sunk in that the problem rested with me and not Carl Reed. The reason I didn't like him was because he was different. I expected him to be exactly like Coach Simmons. They had a lot of similarities but their personalities and approaches to coaching differed considerably. These differences didn't make Coach Reed a bad guy. When I accepted this and tried to understand his approach and philosophy, it all came together. It turned out that he wasn't detached, unapproachable or bull headed. Once I afforded him the time to get to know me, he opened up. Coach Reed's sense of humor pleasantly surprised me along with his wealth of funny stories and witty anecdotes. Even though we graced the hallowed halls of Hazelwood Central some 25 years apart, I related to his Hawk war stories. I laughed at the similarities when I compared his high school shenanigans to mine.

Coach's past came to life when one of his teammates paid us a visit to address our kids. At Hazelwood Central, Carl Reed got to open holes for one of the best fullbacks ever to play for the Hawks, Carey Davis. There weren't many football players on the planet with a better resume. Carey Davis starred at Hazelwood Central and went on to win a Rose Bowl at Illinois along with a Super Bowl ring with the Pittsburgh Steelers. I enjoyed their mutual admiration and relished the chance to pick Carey's brain about Coach Reed's past. Apparently, "Big C", as Carey referred to Carl, played like a beast on the offensive line. Off the field, Carey and Carl were partners in crime who pulled a lot of hijinks that reminded me of my days as a Hawk. These insights into Coach's past, helped to paint a more complete picture of him on a personal level.

Big C's coaching style grew on me too. What I labeled as dictatorial actually reflected solid leadership. Coach Reed, a disciplinarian and perfectionist, demanded that things be done the right way. He allowed no corners to be cut around him. He insisted upon everyone pulling in the same direction; not just the players but the coaching staff too. For example, he refused to tolerate rogue coaches who lost control and got sideways with the refs during a game. He held himself and everyone else to the same high expectations. Somewhat of a micro-manager, Coach Reed didn't share Coach Simmons' willingness to grant significant autonomy to his staff members. But he accepted the responsibility of his leadership style and held himself accountable. Coach Reed didn't point fingers as long as everyone toed the line and held up their end of the bargain.

Coach Reed's tough, disciplinary style belied the fact that he was an old softie on the inside. I think the disciplinarian in him stemmed from his upbringing. Coach, quite young by my standards, piled up a lot of experience in the school of hard knocks over his 35 years. His father, Carl Senior, was an authoritarian figure and held Coach Reed to rigid standards growing up. From the stories he shared, it seemed clear where Carl Junior learned his Spartan ethics. However, Coach Reed didn't despise his father as a cruel task master. He greatly appreciated his dad as a role model and mentor. One time, I asked Carl if his dad was a tough disciplinarian and he replied with a chuckle, "He still is." The look in his eye and the way the corners of his lips curled slightly upward spoke volumes about the love and respect Coach had toward his father.

Carl Reed's coaching style, surely a product of his father's influence, sometimes seemed at odds with his personality. Uncompromising as a coach, he asked no quarter and offered none. He never apologized for a lopsided score and took no exception when the tables were turned. As a human being, he often went to great lengths to help someone in need, even if their predicament was self-inflicted and worthy of chastisement.

Coach Reed's stolid demeanor masked his affection for the kids. What he sometimes lacked in words came shining through in his actions. Take, for example, his *Brady Bunch* family. One of our players, Devin Ruffin, became Coach's stepson by marriage. Their relationship was such that you would never consider Devin to be anything less than his natural son. As a football player though, he treated Devin like the other athletes, no better or worse. I was surprised to learn, late in the season, that another one of our players, Kyrell Roberts, was also Coach Reed's son by adoption. KK, as we called him, became one of my favorite players among the new guys. Beyond being very talented, he brought great heart and spirit to the game. We all fed off of his unbridled enthusiasm. KK and Coach's relationship escaped me due to the difference in their last names and especially the way Coach treated him like everyone else on the team.

Once I found out the full story, I marveled at Coach's Christian charity. KK lived near Coach Reed when he was at Hazelwood West and got to be friends with Devin. Based on their mutual interest in football, they lifted weights together each morning in Coach's basement. Kyrell bounced around a lot, having attended 3 different high schools in 6 months. Kyrell's single mom had a tough time making ends meet. They were evicted from their apartment and Kyrell went to live with an Aunt in Moline Acres, miles away. Unbeknownst to Coach Reed at first, KK got up in the wee hours of the morning and jogged all the way to Coach's house to maintain his weight lifting regimen with Devin. When this came to Coach Reed's attention, he urged KK to move into his home. Later, with the cooperation of Kyrell's mother, he legally adopted him.

Somewhat surprisingly, Coach had nothing bad to say about Kyrell's mother. Rather than condemn her, he understood her plight and maintained a good relationship, just as she did with KK. It amazed me the way Coach willingly accepted this responsibility. Much more than just a financial burden, Coach welcomed the opportunity to make a difference. It astounded me further when I learned that Coach also had a third child, Carl Reed III, whom he called the Tiny Terror. It shouldn't have surprised me considering that Coach Reed had room in his heart for 40 other Crusaders in his care. He treated them all like his adopted children.

Carl possessed a unique outlook toward our players. In light of our Cortez conundrum, I once asked if Coach got frustrated in dealing with all our players' problems. He surprised me by saying, "Kids don't frustrate me. Adults frustrate me. They forget that they were once kids." He added, "Parents can tear a team apart." As we talked in depth, his genuine care for kids was manifested further. Unfortunately, coaching ranks are infested with some hypocrites but Coach Reed's sentiments stood out as authentic when he vowed he preferred good kids to great athletes, if forced to choose between the two. His attitude reflected concern for both the team and the athletes in question. He recognized that, at a college preparatory school like Lutheran North, some students, including great athletes, weren't equipped to handle the academic rigors. Kids who lacked a foundation of academic discipline were doomed to fail. He despised the thought of taking advantage of a young man's superior athletic ability by jeopardizing his future.

He preferred losing them to a public school better equipped with the resources and time necessary to develop remedial students.

Coach Reed grew on me. The coaches he hired and players he accepted in provided the best testimony of his character. Some of the young guys that moved up proved to be a well-spring of talent to replace players we lost to graduation. But plenty of voids remained to be filled by students new to LN. KK stood out in my mind and provided a shot of confidence that the Crusaders would be just fine. Two other newcomers, both freshmen, joined our ranks with KK. It remained to be seen if they were ready to make an immediate impact like Kyrell, a junior. We realized the danger of putting our hopes in mistake-prone freshmen. However, Coach Reed knew we had no other choice, given the size of our squad. He figured that, if we remained patient and tolerant of their growing pains, it would pay dividends later in the season.

Isaiah Azubuike and Isaac Glenn, physically mature for freshmen, both had sturdy, muscular bodies. Blessed with innate talent, their zest for the game impressed us all. In practice and drills they jumped into the fray with reckless abandon. These guys seemed to thrive on contact. Neither could be called a shrinking violet. Surprisingly vocal for freshmen, Isaiah and Isaac displayed an unfettered rah-rah spirit that reflected their true love for the game. I stuck the duo of Isaiah and Isaac with a pet nickname: our young, Prophet Warriors! Despite their obvious talent, neither was brash or cocky but instead remained polite and respectful. The Prophet Warriors behaved like model gentlemen off the field but turned into ferocious tigers once they hit the gridiron.

I was delighted by the way my part-time gig worked out. My football family expanded while I maintained old, familiar ties. The new coaches became brothers like the old crew. Turnover among the players brought blessings too. A new and wonderful tapestry unfolded, revealing a fabric woven with many intriguing and inspiring threads of the next generation of Crusaders. Cam and Berrion proved to be everything I'd expected and more. Their hard work and sacrifices as practice players the year before bore abundant fruit. Malik Mingo and Devin Hart stepped up to bolster our lines anchored by Robert Brown and David Knox. Jordan McDowell and Chris Avery joined the mix and rounded out top notch units on offense and defense.

Jordan Sommerville was ready for prime time as a 2-way terror at slot receiver and safety. Josh Robinson brought his game up a notch and became a stalwart. Dulani Evans delighted me with his progress. He worked hard in the offseason to add upper body strength and brought a new, more aggressive attitude to bear. Dulani looked to put his speed to good use in harassing opposing quarterbacks. Cortez retained some of his Jekyll and Hyde mentality but, for the most part, brought a fresh attitude. That provided good news for us and a scary proposition for opposing defenses.

We lacked depth and needed to play lots of guys both ways but marveled at the wealth of fresh talent we'd gained. We hit the jackpot with some of our transfers but mostly reloaded with returning players who developed during the offseason. Some underclassmen needed seasoning but all seemed ready to take the responsibility of spelling the starters, contributing on special teams and creating competition in practice. Ryan Smith and John Smith blossomed as did Keyshaun Van Dyke. Jackson Ye prepared to put his size to good use. In an odd way, it actually warmed my heart to hear that he got into a scuffle with another student. We deplored bullying but it raised our spirits to see him be the pusher instead of the pushee for once.

Everything seemed to fall into place. Jordan Sommerville didn't fill the vacancy at quarterback but proved to be more valuable as a receiver and safety. Although new to our program as a transfer from Trinity, Aqeel Glass seized the reins of leadership at QB and proved worthy of the challenge. It took a few games for him to get his feet under him but, as the season wore on; the big guy really took control and shined. Once he learned the offense, which Coach Reed had judiciously simplified, things really clicked. Aqeel possessed a strong arm along with a great feel for the game. Although a dual threat, he lacked breakaway speed. However, if the ball rested close to the goal line or we needed a few yards for a first down, he became an irresistible force. Over the course of the season, Aqeel completed the transformation from newbie to a bona fide star. He also toiled as a blue collar quarterback in that he didn't mind getting his hands dirty by playing defensive end too.

Aqeel prospered with Cam, Brandon, Cortez and Jordan, his bevy of talented receivers. Other gifted newcomers waited in the wings in Orece Robinson and Bryce Pease. Questions about our running game lingered. We lost much to graduation but could still run the jet with Cortez or Jordan coming in motion from the slot. However, we needed to reload at tailback and fullback with Martize as the only battle-tested returner. Isaiah, a freshman, and Donovan Marshall, a sophomore, really filled the bill. They, along with Isaac and KK, helped us go from famine to feast in the backfield. A seeming liability became one of our strengths to the point where we employed a backfield by committee to utilize all of our talent.

We banked on a lot of young guys to fill key positions but had all the bases covered. We remained a little shaky until these guys gained some game experience but, in time, our liabilities became assets. Everything came together with one glaring exception. Our kicking game, so vital to success, remained in question. Only one soccer guy offered to pull double duty. With no other choice, we rested our fortunes upon the young, untested shoulders of Tim Branneky, a rather timid sophomore. Although a wonderful kid, Tim seemed to lack a football player's mentality. Kickers usually avoided violent contact but the rigors of pressure packed situations required a certain degree of mental toughness. Tim appeared too gentle to thrive in the sometimes violent, chaotic world of football.

At first, Tim's leg seemed weak for a soccer player. Even his extra points were questionable. Some time passed before we figured out Tim had plenty of leg strength but lacked the confidence necessary to get some oomph behind his kicks. Once he changed his mind set and stopped worrying, the ball flew off his foot. Something still troubled him though. We lacked a solid mesh between kicker and holder. Our regular holder, Brandon Sumrall, remained out for several games while recovering from shoulder surgery. Our depth at wide receiver sufficed without Brandon but it seemed impossible to replace him as our holder. Taking the long snap and getting it down on the kicking block required great hand-eye coordination, super reflexes and soft hands. No one handled this delicate task quite like Brandon and this contributed to our inconsistency in the kicking game. At one point, we considered foregoing extra points altogether in favor of 2-point conversions.

The Crusaders were poised for a championship run despite significant player turnover, a new head coach and several new assistants. We hoped to survive our brutal early schedule as we waited for our young guys to mature. Other challenges arose as 2015 provided a spate of unanticipated maladies of mind, body and spirit. We suffered through typical struggles like injuries, including Brandon's lengthy recovery process. Making grades still plagued some kids and ever present financial problems haunted some of our players' families. With generous, tireless Coach Reed in the lead and the help of LN's Administration and the providence of God, we survived these football foibles. However, we didn't anticipate the ongoing intensity of the Ferguson-Effect.

The influence of the Black Lives Matter movement spread. As other cities like Baltimore bore the brunt of the anger, it seemed to take some heat off of Ferguson. This was a misguided sentiment and provided no solution to the real problem but, frankly, our community welcomed any relief from the constant tension. Even as the focal point shifted, we remained near the spotlight since the false hands up, don't shoot narrative persisted and Ferguson stood as the birthplace of the movement. Things calmed down in Ferguson in 2015 but the sense of being a spark away from another explosion persisted. A sober reminder came on the anniversary of Michael Brown's death on August 9th, 2015. Although non-violent, it showed that emotions still ran high.

When new trouble cropped up in other parts of the country, there always seemed to be some reference to Ferguson. Connecting the dots, so to speak, remained top of mind and fueled the movement. This bothered me the most. Why couldn't people think rationally and take each incident on a case-by-case basis? The shooting of Sam Dubose by a University of Cincinnati police officer in July 2015 seemed like excessive force to me and a case where the officer needed to be indicted and tried. Likewise, when Laquan McDonald was shot 16 times by Chicago police officer Jason Van Dyke in October 2014, it appeared that a criminal injustice had occurred. As these cases dragged on throughout 2015, the Black Lives Matter movement couldn't separate them for judgment on their own merits. They were linked to Michael Brown, Freddie Gray and all the others as part of a systematic movement afoot by police everywhere to target young black men. I disagreed with the underlying premise. The lesson learned from the Michael Brown case and others was, in my opinion, to respect the police and remain compliant during arrest procedures. If an injustice occurred, it needed to be taken up in court later through proper legal channels.

Although the movement remained top of mind for many Americans, it didn't dominate discussion at LN or slow down our football aspirations. Still, not many weeks passed without the St. Louis Post-Dispatch reporting something related to the Ferguson- Effect. Stories popped up even late into the year. December 16th brought news of a lawsuit filed by protestors against a County ordinance related to police actions allowed during protests. They claimed the new law was too vague in that it allowed police to arrest protestors for interfering with or obstructing the police "in any manner." The media issued a litany of other stories that kept the Ferguson-Effect from fading away. Race relations stayed in our national consciousness throughout

2015 and the subject remained pertinent if not top of mind at LN.

It really hit home when the movement took to college campuses across the nation. I didn't care so much what happened at Yale or other such far-flung places but it grabbed my attention when Mizzou took center stage in early November. I chaffed when the situation called Mizzou's academic credentials into question and became sorely disappointed when it engulfed the Tiger football program. Mizzou football already suffered with a dismal season and this heaped sour icing on a putrid cake. After a couple of isolated, largely unsubstantiated incidents, protestors with the aid of the media used the purported indiscretions to condemn the entire University of Missouri as a home to systematic racial injustice. This stung me because I personally knew this to be untrue. Undeterred by the facts, Black Lives Matter, et al took over the quadrangle and it became a media spectacle. Then, a minority of about 30 members of the football team voiced their support for the protestors and turned things into a real circus.

Astonishingly, head football coach, Gary Pinkel, tweeted out his support for the movement. As a football coach, my first thought was, *no wonder Mizzou is having a losing season. Their priorities are all out of whack.* Shortly thereafter, I was flabbergasted when the President, Tim Wolfe, and Chancellor, R. Bowen Loftin, resigned their posts. Later this led to Gary Pinkel's resignation after 15 years even though he cited health concerns as the basis for his decision.

The world, my world, had truly gone mad. Some bad elements within the movement showed their true colors at Mizzou. During one rally, the black members of the movement asked the white supporters to leave the room so they could conduct private discussions. I thought, *so much for racial harmony*. Later, some members of the movement had the gall to complain when the media attention shifted away from Columbia, Missouri to Paris, France after the terrorist attacks that left hundreds of people dead or maimed. This seemed unbelievably hypocritical and grossly narcissistic on their part but it actually happened.

Life went on at Lutheran North regardless of everything else that transpired around us. Ferguson survived despite the lingering Ferguson- Effect. Yet things never settled down completely due to the media coverage of periodic flare-ups of unrest elsewhere. In one instance, a mistrial was declared in December in the case of the first officer tried in the Freddie Gray case in Baltimore. As Chicago proceeded toward the trial of Officer Van Dyke, angry protesters demanded the resignation of Mayor

Rahm Emanuel. Late in December, the spotlight turned to Cleveland when the Grand Jury declined to bring charges against the officer who shot 12-year-old Tamir Rice. They deemed it justifiable self-defense since the toy gun brandished by the youngster could not be distinguished from the real thing. Our nation seemed more divided than ever as we maneuvered through 2015 but the bond of fellowship at North remained firm and sure despite the adversity we faced and all the changes that took place among our staff, players and student body.

Other trials closer to home tested our mettle more than any of the aforementioned external influences. None proved more heart-rending than the tragedy our fellow coach, Jon Mueller, and his wife, Jamie, encountered. With a mix of joy and trepidation after their miscarriage in March, they conceived another child 2 months later. As might be expected, they were nervous, especially Jamie. However, this time, the pregnancy proceeded and they eagerly anticipated another bouncing baby boy. Weeks passed, the tension subsided and Jon and Jamie looked forward to a joyous addition to their family. Then, their world turned upside down at 19 weeks.

During a routine checkup, an ultrasound revealed an unusual amount of fluid around the baby's abdomen. They received the devastating diagnosis that the baby suffered with hydrops fetalis. Some research and discussions with the doctors revealed this could indicate a myriad of serious problems including heart defects, severe anemia or developmental/genetic defects. Joy turned to fear and consternation. We all shared these feelings since the Muellers formed part of our extended family and our prayers abounded.

The next 3 weeks were excruciatingly difficult. Some of the medical personnel suggested an abortion, something out of the question for Jon and Jamie under any circumstances. Thankfully, others presented more practical suggestions that offered a modicum of hope. An avalanche of responsibility accompanied their optimism. They had to face some nearly impossible decisions. A battery of tests revealed that the baby suffered from severe anemia. After numerous doctor visits, it boiled down to one key decision. If they allowed nature to take its course, little Jackson Aaron Mueller, might remain in the womb long enough to have a fighting chance for survival after pre-mature birth. Otherwise, PUBS treatments in the womb might extend the pregnancy. This entailed blood transfusions to baby Jackson. Both paths involved significant risks but Jon and Jamie couldn't sit on the fence for long.

After hours and days of deliberations, prayers and soul searching, they opted for the transfusions.

This seemed to offer the best chance of helping little Jackson in his fight to achieve viability outside the womb. This meant more difficult, stress-filled procedures but, thankfully, they succeeded, not once but 3 times. Then, despite everyone's best efforts, the medical procedures failed and Jamie gave birth to stillborn Jackson Aaron Mueller who was called home to glory on September 29th, 2015. The forlorn parents barely mustered the strength to introduce Jared to his baby brother and gave Jackson a proper burial. The Mueller's great faith was manifested through this and many other courageous acts. In spite of their devastating temporal loss, they looked forward with all certainty to a grand and glorious reunion with Jackson in heaven.

The faith in action demonstrated by Jon and Jamie might best be summed up with 2 scripture passages they circulated publicly at the beginning and end of their difficult ordeal. At the onset they posted Psalm 139:13-16, "For thou hast possessed my reins: thou hast covered me in my mother's womb. I will praise thee; for I am fearfully and wonderfully made: marvelous are thy works; and that my soul knoweth right well. My substance was not hid from thee, when I was made in secret, and curiously wrought in the lowest parts of the earth. Thine eyes did see my substance, yet being imperfect; and in thy book all my members were written, which in continuance were fashioned, when as yet there was none of them." Upon his passing, they posted Isaiah 43:1 and substituted Jackson's name for Jacob's, "But now thus saith the LORD that created thee, O *Jackson*, and he that formed thee, O *Jackson*, Fear not: for I have redeemed thee, I have called thee by thy name; thou art mine."

We suffered many hardships in 2015 but none affected us more profoundly than the loss of baby Jackson. The tragedy taught us to view our temporal sorrows with spiritual discernment. Our brother and sister, Jon and Jamie, truly inspired us with expressions of peace and faith that could not have been possible apart from God. His gentle hand lifted the Muellers and us all. This reassured us in the midst of our anguish. It drew us closer together as a team and a school. For the sake of the team, Jon tried to disguise his lingering heartache as best he could but nothing completely masked the harsh reality of the situation. No one lived through such a tragedy with their outlook and priorities unchanged.

As we absorbed this tragedy, our reconstructed, fledgling football team seemed to come apart at the seams. We opened at home on August 22nd against Clayton and suffered a demoralizing loss 29-21. Normally, we could have bounced back against Principia. However, when they dropped football it left a hole in our schedule that we filled with St. Louis University High School, one of the best, large school programs in the area. It seemed like suicide but proved necessary given the short notice we received from Principia. We played the game under the lights on Friday night at their house. With our young guys and new quarterback ill prepared for this challenge so early in the season, SLUH trounced us 48-13. Things didn't get any easier the next week as we traveled to Westminster. Loaded again, the Wildcats stuffed us 35-6. .

This seemed like a replay of 2013 but Brian Simmons' steady hand didn't rest on the helm. The dire situation called for Carl Reed to show his true colors. Our nose dive tested his character and drew upon his experience. He possessed plenty of both for someone only 35 years old.

He played left guard at Austin Peay and started his coaching career in football and basketball at Northeast High School in Clarksville, Tennessee. He moved on to Pioneer Christian Academy in Nashville as head coach and won a state championship in basketball. From there, he served as a camp counsellor at the prestigious IMG Academy in football-rich Bradenton, Florida. After one more stop in Tennessee at Memphis' Melrose High School, Coach Reed headed back to St. Louis as the head football coach at University City High

School. Thereafter, he became the head coach at Hazelwood West before he found his way to Lutheran North. Carl Reed faced plenty of adversity along the way.

My new, positive attitude toward Coach Reed was reinforced by what I witnessed from him in action. Never one to get rattled, Coach's unshakable confidence in the midst of our pitiful losing streak helped us stay the course. Coach never conceded our goal of a championship season. Given our winless record and spotty play, this seemed ludicrous but something in his demeanor convinced us otherwise. During this time, Jon and Jamie's troubles really took a toll on Coach Mueller. The consternation over Baby Jackson's condition and repeated doctor visits and consultations diverted Jon's attention from his Offensive Coordinator duties. Always a man of action, Coach Reed offered more than advice and consolation. Along with his other responsibilities, he took the offensive reins and called the plays on game days.

In our fourth game, we faced another good opponent, Priory, on the road. Coach instilled new confidence in our young charges that day. We started fast and built upon that momentum throughout the contest. Coach Reed shattered his image as a conservative play caller. Although he preferred a run-first approach, he showed his willingness and ability to do whatever it took to succeed. He pulled out all the stops and launched a shock and awe air attack. Aqeel responded marvelously to this opportunity as did Cam and our host of other talented receivers. We won going away, 50-0. Some of Priory's coaches took exception to the lopsided score but they misconstrued Coach Reed's intention. After 3 demoralizing losses, he wanted our young guys to learn to execute for 4 quarters and regain our shattered confidence.

Our schedule remained brutal. On the road for the fourth straight week, we faced the John Burroughs Bombers, again ranked number 1 among area small schools. Eager for revenge, they hoped to reciprocate for the beating we administered to them in 2014. The day started poorly with some bad breaks and snowballed from there. We looked like a different team than the one that handily defeated Priory the week before. Our swagger deserted us and we played like a bunch of young, inexperienced, disorganized kids. We left with our tails between our legs after a humiliating 53-12 defeat. Unflappable, Coach Reed didn't rant or rave. He calmly offered this simple assessment: we needed improvement and a good week of practice.

It seemed that nothing deterred the Crusaders; not the Ferguson- Effect or even the worst of tragedies like the death of baby Jackson that happened around this time. Unbowed by the Burroughs pasting, we finally came back to LN for homecoming against our sister rival, Lutheran South. Better than ever, Cody Schrader served as a one-man wrecking crew who almost single-handedly vanquished us. They scored at will but we cranked up our offense and pulled out all the stops. We matched our single game scoring record to seize victory at 72-65. Next, we dispatched a game MICDS team 33-21 at Lamothe Field. Back on the road and under the lights, we faced Trinity, our neighborhood rival with the knack for mounting furious comebacks against us. Aqeel had other ideas in mind for his former teammates. We walked away with a convincing 40-14 win. Then we closed the regular season on a roll with a resounding 69-19 win at St. Mary's.

Just as Coach Reed predicted, by season's end our new QB and all of our young guys came into their own. This included our jittery kicker. Once acclimated and teamed with sure-handed Brandon as his holder, Tim Branneky kicked with confidence and proved he possessed a strong, reliable leg. By season's end, TB became almost automatic and eliminated any thoughts of 2-point conversions. Despite his shaky start, Tim showed amazing growth and ended in 5th place for the most extra points in LN history with 45. Additionally, he set a school record for extra points in a playoff game with 10 against Northwest Academy. Timid Tim became Bold Branneky.

We rolled into the district playoffs on a high note and didn't miss a beat. We obliterated Northwest Academy 72-0 and then beat the farm boys from Hermann going away, 56-22. Then, as if history was repeating itself, we faced an undefeated Brentwood team on their soggy field under the lights on November 6th. The Eagles featured a fantastic running back, Jacob Clay, who resembled South's Cody Schrader. Stopping the stellar running back seemed next to impossible so our offense picked up the gauntlet. Aqeel and company shined in eclipsing a strong performance by Brentwood's offense to secure a 64-38 victory.

Somehow, despite massive turnover, a new head coach and quarterback, a coaching staff makeover, reliance on a bunch of wet-behind-the-ears underclassmen and tons of adversity, the Crusaders became District Champs again and headed to the state quarterfinals.

In football parlance, a Ferguson Miracle didn't happen. Some may have deemed it a miracle if we had swept our way to the Dome and knocked off Goliath Lamar to become state champs. Like the year before, we faced Palmyra in the quarterfinals but, this time, at home. On a beautiful fall Saturday on November 14th at Lamothe Field, everything seemed perfect for us to exact our revenge on the Panthers. Unfortunately, only one team showed up at the sound of the first whistle. The first half was a disaster. Palmyra came out breathing fire and the Crusaders looked like Dr. Evil had stolen our mojo. Once our heads stopped spinning and we looked up at the scoreboard, we trailed 28-0 at half-time. We gathered on the grassy hillside behind the far end zone and waited for a tongue lashing from Coach Reed but it never happened. Instead, he calmly went about the business of instilling the confidence we'd lost. Quietly, he raised our spirits and determination drew across our faces.

We played like a different team in the second half. The Crusaders controlled the line of scrimmage and the tempo. Our first score brought cheers and some needed relief from our embarrassment. As we crept closer, we regained more than respect. We entertained the notion that we could actually stage an improbable if not impossible comeback. Everyone played 100% better than in the first half. The whole team morphed from Hyde to Jekyll including Cortez Simmons. He played an integral part in our furious comeback by scoring 3 TDs. Unfortunately, our fairy tale finish fell short. We turned a rout into a real barn burner but, in the end, Palmyra held on for a 38-28 victory. Our season ended well short of our highest aspirations.

It seemed fitting that we didn't conclude our season with a gridiron miracle. It might have detracted from the real story at 5401 Lucas & Hunt Road. What I witnessed in 2013 and 2014 transcended football. When I stayed on in 2015 it added an exclamation point. People, names and faces changed along with our circumstances and it proved that nothing lasted forever in this crazy world. However, the most important aspect of life at Lutheran North remained constant: Jesus Christ and His inspired, inerrant, powerful, life-giving word of truth. "Jesus Christ the same yesterday, and today, and forever" (Hebrews 13:8). "Heaven and earth shall pass away, but my words shall not pass away" (Matthew 24:35).

God's legacy of providence continued at Lutheran North despite all the other changes that occurred in 2015. Brian Simmons, Kelvin Austin, Matt Hieke and, in part, I had moved on. Newcomers filled the void: Reed, Randle, Powell, Davis and Pomerenke. Some 20 players graduated, young ones stepped up and new ones joined the fray. Although the Ferguson- Effect persisted, other difficulties faded as new problems surfaced to add to our challenges. Yet, through it all, God never abandoned us. To the contrary, He continued to shower us with his grace, mercy, forgiveness and salvation.

Why did such providence continue? Simply put, Lutheran North maintained its reverence and respect for God's word. It remained a staple of our spiritual diet. "Then said Jesus to those Jews which believed on him, If ye continue in my word, then are ye my disciples indeed; and ye shall know the truth, and the truth shall make you free" (John 8:31-32).

For me, Lutheran North provided many wonderful blessings. That I gained new brothers and sisters in Christ in the unique bond of true fellowship surely filled the bill and the kids occupied a special place on this list. There isn't enough space here for me to recount all the wonderful memories I accumulated through our kids. But these 2 examples are reflective of the many uplifting experiences I enjoyed.

Jeremy Bowen, our quiet, hulking center graduated in 2014/2015. He provided a great example of why a book shouldn't be judged by the cover. The seemingly shy introvert showed himself to be actually quite outgoing. In the summer after graduation he served as a camp counselor for kids and also wrote articles about the St. Louis Rams for a local blog spot. He demonstrated that still waters run deep when he sent me the following thank you note after graduation.

"Coach S,

Thank you very much for the generous card and gift. But more importantly, thank you for everything you've done for me the last two years. From all of the devotions to you pushing me around asking if I was ready for that nose tackle from Burroughs and whatnot. I cherished it all. The one that stuck with me the most was the devotion after the Panther game about how important faith is and that there is more to life than football. Thank you very much. God Bless.

Jeremy Bowen"

This one came late in 2015 from an unexpected source. Orece Robinson, a freshman, didn't start and didn't get much playing time. Nevertheless, he caught my eye in practice and warm-ups before our games. He always gave 100% and never dropped a pass. Before the district playoffs began, I purchased new gloves for all of our starting receivers. In a rare exception, I also bought a pair for Orece. When I gave them to him privately, I told him I made an exception because of his effort and consistency in practice. Furthermore, in an attempt to boost his confidence for the future, I told him I felt he had the right stuff to fill Cam and Brandon's shoes when they graduated. In a fateful coincidence due to the lopsided score, we inserted Orece into our first playoff game against Northwest Academy after half-time. Not satisfied to run out the clock, Orece sprinted flat out on a deep corner route, launched his body parallel to the ground and hauled in a long, circus reception. The freshman's efforts evoked wild cheers from our veterans on the sidelines. Much to my astonishment and sheer delight, Orece trotted past me after the game and whispered, "That one was for you Coach." It brought a tear to my eye.

Such were the treasures of coaching. Long-time veterans like Simmons and Reed often expressed the same sentiment. Wins and trophies didn't provide the best memories. A coach's greatest gifts were supplied through the gratitude of players and their lifelong accomplishments on and off the field.

Outsiders naturally considered North's location a major drawback due to the constant turmoil that surrounded our idyllic sanctuary. This view was reinforced by the economic challenges faced by some of our families. I disagreed and wouldn't have changed our location or demographics for anything. The Ferguson- Effect created some unfortunate consequences but the blessings far outweighed the negatives and we treasured our students regardless of their economic standing. Thankfully, due to my personal involvement within the safe and peaceful confines of Lutheran North, I saw both sides of the equation clearly and avoided undue influence from the media's narrative.

My close, lifelong familiarity with Ferguson shaped my outlook too. I recognized how things changed and abhorred the looting, burning, violence and hatred but felt these things represented the exception rather than the rule. I understood the universal nature of sin and evil along with the foolishness of casting stones at others. Ferguson included some bad apples, perhaps outsiders, but many people simply sought a public forum for needed reforms. In that regard, I found Ferguson to be no different than any other community where people sought a better life for their families.

I felt that any admonishments should be directed elsewhere, not toward the people of Ferguson. The media fanned the flames of unrest for ratings sake. Feckless leaders too often sought political gains over safety, security and meaningful reforms. Some police, a small minority, used poor judgment and let ill will guide their actions. Some protesters selfishly sought the limelight or opportunistically seized the situation to vent evil rage. A smaller, more violent subset turned to vigilantism against the police. Unfortunately, some were ambushed and gunned down for no reason other than the uniforms they wore.

The root cause of such evil escaped most observers. In our secularized society, many turned to flawed, fickle, corrupt and unreliable human reason. Too often, this shaped opinions and actions regarding race relations in 21st Century America. People rejected God and turned away from His holy word. With this as our path, we're doomed to continued turmoil, hatred, racism and divisions.

We need not be dismayed though, for "The Lord God omnipotent still reigns" (Revelation 19:6). True peace, love, joy, hope, forgiveness and salvation are found wherever God's word is revered. As always, God still intervenes in the affairs of people this way. God's miraculous intercession in the lives of His people, while not as overt as in Old Testament times, continues through His means of grace: word and sacrament.

As I was privileged to see firsthand, proof positive shined through at Lutheran High School North

God performed a great and mighty miracle at Lutheran North; the Ferguson Miracle. He painted a bold portrait in contrasting colors that could only be viewed through spiritual lenses. An incredible beam of light pierced through the surrounding shades of gloom. In the midst of a maelstrom of sin and hatred, God blessed Lutheran North with the bonds of fellowship in Jesus Christ.

We were led to follow Christ Jesus' example in two godly principles that defied the chaotic scenes and secular pressures that surrounded us. We practiced human relations on a personal level, from the heart, rather than race relations from afar. Most importantly, we put our trust in the Lord and revered God's word in the Bible as the source of authority and truth in all things.

Humanly speaking, we should have succumbed to the overwhelming influence of the Ferguson-effect. Yet, Lutheran North remained a peaceful sanctuary. In worldly terms, this defied all logic. Yet God intervened to accomplish the impossible.

Our communities, country and world are so plagued with strife and divisions, our doom seems inevitable. Still there is hope. If we repent and turn back to God in Christ, we can share in the legacy that lives on at Lutheran High School North near Ferguson, Missouri. The legacy consists of the special bond that is summarized in these two sets of passages:

Romans 12:1-6

"I beseech you therefore, brethren, by the mercies of God, that ye present your bodies a living sacrifice, holy, acceptable unto God, which is your reasonable service. And be not conformed to this world: but be ye transformed by the renewing of your mind, that ye may prove what is that good, and acceptable, and perfect, will of God. For I say, through the grace given unto me, to every man that is among you, not to think of himself more highly than he ought to think; but to think soberly, according as God hath dealt to every man the measure of faith. For as we have many members in one body, and all members have not the same office: So we, being many, are one body in Christ, and every one members one of another. Having then gifts differing according to the grace that is given to us."

Galatians 3:23-29

"But before faith came, we were kept under the law, shut up unto the faith which should afterwards be revealed. Wherefore the law was our schoolmaster to bring us unto Christ, that we might be justified by faith. But after that faith is come, we are no longer under a schoolmaster. For ye are all the children of God by faith in Christ Jesus. For as many of you as have been baptized into Christ have put on Christ. There is neither Jew nor Greek, there is neither bond nor free, there is neither male nor female: for ye are all one in Christ Jesus. And if ye be Christ's, then are ye Abraham's seed, and heirs according to the promise."

There are many reasons to be pessimistic about our future. Evil is ever present and floods our homes through the media on a daily basis. Race relations in our communities and country seem at an all-time low. Yet the spirit of optimism is still passed down from one generation to the next. The kindness and grace of Stan Musial did not die with his passing and is not bound by skin color. It lives on in the likes of his successor, another St. Louis treasure, Lou Brock.

People are incredibly frustrated, frightened and angry. This is clearly evident in our political climate. This has simultaneously stirred dangerous and wholesome emotions that are accompanied by ugly conflict and lively hope. There's a clarion call from many quarters to make America great again. This can be a worthy cause, if viewed in the right light … through spiritual lenses.

We won't achieve this purpose through military might, political pressure or even social reforms. If we want to make America great again, we need to make America good again. This seems impossible because we have lost our moral compass. We have turned our backs on the only true source of goodness in this world: God. Can we turn back to

God in Jesus Christ and look again, in reverence, to His inspired, inerrant word for our guidance and edification? This would surely take a miracle. But miracles can and do happen by the power and grace of God. I know this is true because I witnessed it myself at Lutheran North where God's love still stands in stark contrast to human nature.

307 | Steve Stranghoener

APPENDIX

What is a miracle?

If you look up the word miracle, there are so many definitions you might believe it would take a miracle to get it right. This one, offered by Merriam-Webster, provides a good jumping off point: an extraordinary event manifesting divine intervention in human affairs. Although "extraordinary" might be somewhat vague, I think this definition contains the key elements.

Miracles occur when Almighty God intervenes in our lives in a way that contravenes the laws of nature.

Even this seemingly stark demarcation can fall short. People make a habit of labeling natural phenomena as miraculous. Take, for example, a triple play in baseball or a last second comeback in football via a Hail Mary touchdown pass. Life is full of astounding absurdities and nearly incalculable coincidences. Nevertheless, beating the odds, no matter how long they may be, doesn't necessarily constitute a miracle. Dumb luck is not an indicator of God's intervention in our affairs.

Sometimes it's hard to discern miracles. There was a news report in July 2015 that a Massachusetts man named Eugene Finney was on vacation with his family in Huntington Beach, CA when he was attacked by a shark. It stunned him and left him with some nasty cuts but nothing severe enough to prompt him to go to the hospital. Apparently, the shark rammed him much harder than he bit him because Eugene later experienced chest pains that forced him to reconsider. Once in the hospital, they found that he had suffered blunt force trauma to his thoracic cavity. In running the tests, they inadvertently discovered a cancerous tumor about the size of a walnut on his right kidney. This allowed the doctors to remove the tumor at an early onset before it reached a fatal stage. Eugene declared that his unfortunate encounter with the shark was a blessing in disguise, one that gave him a second chance at life.

Was this a miracle or just an incredibly felicitous coincidence? Eugene didn't attribute his good fortune to his faith in God. Miracles are not dependent on the beliefs of people. We know from the Bible that some people refused to believe in Christ in spite of His miracles.

In one of many examples, we're told in John 12:37, "But though he had done so many miracles before them, yet they believed not on him." If God intervened in the encounter between Mr. Finney and the shark, He did so for a good purpose that transcends just saving life and limb. If so, something of a spiritual nature will be revealed in time.

While divining miracles can be an imponderable task, we have scads of examples that leave nothing to doubt. Jesus turned water into wine and walked upon the water. He made the blind to see, deaf to hear, mute to speak and lame to walk. He cured the lepers of their dread disease. Christ drove out evil angels from people who were demon-possessed. Jesus calmed the winds and the waves by His voice alone. He even raised people from the dead on several occasions, most notably, His friend Lazarus. This was done in front of many eyewitnesses after Lazarus had been decomposing in his tomb for 4 days to the point there was a stench. It doesn't get any plainer than that, does is? Even Christ's enemies recognized this as a miracle. Still it didn't sway the hard-hearted, hypocritical religious leaders who were only concerned with maintaining their own status. They didn't deny the miracle but plotted as to how they might overcome Jesus' influence among the people. In John 11:47 we're told, "Then gathered the chief priests and the Pharisees a council, and said, what do we? For this man doeth many miracles."

Miracles aren't limited to the person of Jesus Christ. Even after His death, resurrection and ascension into heaven ... all miracles of the highest order ... the Apostles were able to perform many similar, amazing miracles by the power of the Holy Spirit. Prior to His incarnation in the person of Jesus, God performed many astounding miracles in Old Testament times that were undeniably His work. The plagues visited upon Egypt and the parting of the Red Sea still resonate today as immortalized in film. The imagination of man cannot conjure greater theater and drama. It seemed God was always preserving His people in spectacular, phenomenal ways. Moses was rescued from certain death under Pharaoh's orders as a tiny baby and plucked from out of the river's reeds only to be later raised up to dizzying heights of power at Pharaoh's side.

Years later, every Hebrew baby was spared from death during the first Passover. Joseph's brothers meant it for evil when they sold him into slavery but God intended it for good. Joseph suffered a roller coaster ride of highs and lows but eventually amassed so much power and influence in Egypt that he was able to save his family and many others from a terrible 7-year famine. Isaac was spared when God provided a ram caught in a thicket to serve as Abraham's sacrifice.

Based on these examples, can we conclude that God's supernatural intervention into our affairs always accrues to our benefit in a temporal sense? No, it only takes a few well-known recollections to prove otherwise. Sometimes, God metes out His wrath and judgment in miraculous ways. Surely the Egyptians felt differently about the miraculous plagues than did the Hebrews. The fire and brimstone that rained down upon Sodom and Gomorrah destroyed everything in its path. Then, of course, there was the Great Flood. It engulfed the entire sin-infested world. The only survivors were 8 people, Noah and his family, and the animals they were instructed to take on the ark.

Some would argue, and rightfully so, that even these massive tragedies provided hidden blessings from God. Yet, there's no denying that the objects of God's judgment would beg to differ. So, are God's miracles a blessing, curse or both? This we know for certain: God is not the author of evil and He takes no pleasure in the death of the wicked (Ezekiel 33:11). Thus, we can conclude that God is not responsible for the troubles besetting this sin-sick world of ours, unless He cites specific acts in His word according to His wise and purposeful judgment. Otherwise, our tragedies and disasters must be laid at our own feet as the natural consequence of man's sins rather than some kind of divine retribution. Christ has already suffered our punishment for us. But God can use even these unfortunate things to serve His good and loving purposes for us.

Before we move forward, let's take a moment to address another question. Can we conclude that miracles tend to be overt manifestations of God's omnipotent power? From many of the examples noted above we might say yes. But, unmistakably, this is not always true. Take the case of God's prophet, Elijah. In one respect, there was no denying the way God inserted Himself into Elijah's life and actions. Crowds of people came out to see the battle between God's prophet and the Prophets of Baal and the Prophets of the Groves. They squared off to see whose deity was the real God. The odds were 850-1 against Elijah, not to mention that the former had the power and might of King Ahab and Queen Jezebel behind them.

By the power of the Holy Spirit, Elijah's confidence didn't wane in the face of such a steep disadvantage. He even ridiculed the Prophets of Baal as they wailed to their false god to manifest himself. Elijah mocked and chided them to speak up since Baal was obviously snoozing and couldn't hear them. Then he put on a show, with God's help, that put P. T. Barnum to shame. He doused his altar with 12 barrels of water so that everything was soaked and the water overflowed and filled the trench around it. Yet God left no doubt in the minds of any of the onlookers when he rained down such fire that it consumed the wood, animal sacrifice, all the water and even the 12 rocks that formed Elijah's altar. Then he empowered Elijah to kill all of the false prophets.

You might ask if this is not more evidence of how easy it is to discern a real miracle of God. Well, let's not forget the rest of the story. Wicked Queen Jezebel was not deterred when she heard of the flashy show of force from Elijah and the true, Triune God. She had killed many of God's prophets before and vowed to do the same to Elijah. What happened to God's heroic champion when he was faced with Jezebel's deadly threat and leaned upon his own understanding instead of the promises of God? He looked around and saw that, from an earthly standpoint, he was all alone against the overwhelming might that Queen Jezebel could muster. He high-tailed it like a scared rabbit and hid out in the wilderness, in a cave. Did God come to his rescue by sending legions of angels to slay Jezebel's forces? Did He send lightning bolts to decimate their ranks? Did God buoy Elijah's confidence by giving him a pep talk in a thunderous voice from heaven in front of hordes of terrified onlookers? No, He came to Elijah in that barren cave with no witnesses around and spoke to him in a still, small voice. He quietly assured Elijah that he wasn't alone. There were still 7,000 in Israel that had not bowed the knee to Baal.

Sometimes God's miracles are full of flash and flamboyance but other times not so much. They often are manifested in obvious blessings and benefits but at other times are accompanied by what can only seem like curses associated with His wrath and judgment. However, most tragedies and disasters, be they fires, famines, plagues, hurricanes, floods, mass shootings, terror attacks, tornadoes or the like, have nothing to do with God but instead are the consequence of man's sinfulness. Some occurrences that seem extraordinary are nothing more than dumb luck, incredible misfortune or astounding coincidences. Miracles don't necessarily involve Christians exclusively. We can't see into anyone's heart and we certainly can't read the future to tell who may be part of God's elect but are still awaiting the gift of God-given faith.

This may seem disheartening. It could lead one to believe that the only confirmed miracles are those recorded for us in the Bible. However, this is not the case. Miracles are still occurring today. God is still intervening in the lives of people every moment of every day. Although He is only limited by Himself, God most often operates in a way today that doesn't appear very miraculous. Sometimes God is not very conspicuous and His miracles can go completely unnoticed. Often they can only be discerned through spiritual lenses.

This example from Scripture can offer some illumination. Do you recall the story of how the King of Syria encompassed the city of Dothan with his army in order to trap and kill the Prophet Elisha who had been providing the King of Israel with God-given guidance to thwart the Syrian's plans for conquest? Elisha's servant saw how they were surrounded and was naturally distraught while Elisha remained as cool as a cucumber. The servant was looking at things with temporal eyesight while Elisha was fixed with spiritual lenses. Elisha tried to comfort his servant as recorded in 2 Kings 6:16, "And he answered, Fear not: for they that be with us are more than they that be with them." This must have thrown the panic-stricken servant for a loop. They were only two against thousands. Then Elisha fitted his servant with spiritual lenses according to the next verse, "And Elisha prayed, and said, LORD, I pray thee open his eyes that he may see. And the LORD opened the eyes of the young man; and he saw: and, behold, the mountain was full of horses and chariots of fire round about Elisha."

Now that's what I call a miracle! Yet, the servant would have never sensed a thing under normal, natural circumstances. This is more relevant today than ever, since God has chosen to work through His means of grace: His word and sacraments connected to His word.

All of those flashy, flamboyant miracles recorded in Scripture served specific purposes of God. Why did God save Noah and his family? It was necessary to keep His promise of the coming Savior. The same was true for Abraham and Isaac. God preserved His plan of salvation through the specific lineage He had vowed. What was the point of the whole, long saga involving Joseph from his teen years to his 30s? Was it just to stave off the consequences of a pending famine? No. The ultimate good that God intended (Genesis 50:20) was to preserve the Savior's line through Joseph's brother Judah. Even the destruction of Sodom and Gomorrah held a silver lining of salvation for Lot and his family ... except for his salty wife. She was still viewing things through worldly glasses and brought about her own doom like the other inhabitants for whom she longed.

Everything God does in our lives has one overarching purpose. That is, to carry out His plan of salvation for us. That's the one thing that ties everything together including God's miracles.

Christ revealed as much in the Bible. Look at John 2:11, "This beginning of miracles did Jesus in Cana of Galilee, and manifested forth his glory; and his disciples believed on him." Next read John 14:11, "Believe me that I am in the Father, and the Father in me: or else believe me for the very works' sake." Jesus said, in effect, the proof is in the pudding, look at my miracles. He didn't perform these miracles for the purpose of self-aggrandizement. God didn't need to puff Himself up. He did these things for our benefit, so that we might believe in Him and look to Him for forgiveness and salvation.

This grace of God was not reserved for believers only. It extended to all, even enemies such as the Pharisees. Look at how this motivated one of their own to seek out the Lord. We read in John 3:1-2, "There was a man of the Pharisees, named Nicodemus, a ruler of the Jews: The same came to Jesus by night, and said unto him, Rabbi, we know that thou art a teacher come from God: for no man can do these miracles that thou does, except God be with him."

Before His ascension, Christ promised to empower His apostles for the same purpose. That is, He wanted to establish their authority so that people would believe in the message they carried from Him. After exhorting Philip to believe in Him because of the miraculous work He had done (John 14:11), Jesus followed up in the next verse with this promise. "Verily, verily, I say unto you, He that believeth on me, the works that I do shall he do also; and greater works than these shall he do; because I go unto my Father."

There it is. Jesus explained that the apostles would receive great power in order to carry on His work of spreading the good news of salvation. In verse 13 Jesus goes further in offering this hope to you and me today, "And whatsoever ye shall ask in my name, that will I do, that the Father may be glorified in the Son." Wow, we too have miraculous power at our disposal through prayer.

You might wonder why we don't see God's miraculous power manifested so boldly then today. But there is no need to fret, brothers and sisters. We only need to put on our spiritual spectacles to see that there are still miracles abounding everywhere. There is a good reason why miracles are manifested differently today than they were in Old Testament times. God has elected to work through His means of grace in this New Covenant age. Why would God need to manifest Himself in such ostentatious ways today? He has already revealed Himself in the most overt way possible. He came to earth and clothed Himself in human flesh so we could see Him and know Him intimately in the person of Jesus Christ.

Christ provided the fulfillment of all of those Messianic promises delivered under the Old Covenant.

What is needed to believe in Jesus Christ as Savior? Must we see Him or His servants heal the sick, speak in tongues, show all manner of signs and wonders or perform exorcisms? Must we see the resurrection of Christ anew? No. Christ has already come. He completed the work of salvation on the Cross of Calvary. The proof positive was sealed for all time in the glorious resurrection of our Lord. All of this has been recorded for our edification in the Holy Bible. It contains everything necessary for our salvation.

We are saved, the Bible tells us in Ephesians 2:8-9 through God-given faith which is a free gift … "For by grace are ye saved through faith; and that not of yourselves: it is the gift of God: Not of works, lest any man should boast." And how do we get this faith? We simply turn to the Scriptures as it says in Romans 10:17 … "So then faith cometh by hearing, and hearing by the word of God."

Finally, how are we fed spiritually and kept in saving Christian faith unto life everlasting? Christ's instructions are recorded for us in John 8:31-32, "Then said Jesus to those Jews which believed on him, If ye continue in my word, then are ye my disciples indeed; And ye shall know the truth, and the truth shall make you free."

This seems so simple and such an unassuming way to achieve eternal life and salvation, but don't be fooled by humility and meekness. The very word of God is so much more than ink, paper and binding. It is, in and of itself, one of the greatest miracles God has ever set before the eyes of man. It is the inspired, inerrant truth of God revealed to man by the power of the Holy Spirit. It has been miraculously preserved against all manner of powerful foes throughout the ages and will remain intact even after the present heavens and earth are burned up by God on the final day of judgment when Christ returns (Matthew 24:35). The word of God is the very power of God unto salvation to everyone that believes (Romans 1:16). The word is Jesus Christ, the Incarnate Word, in power and essence (John 1:14). Yes, the same power that was used to perform all of those astounding miracles of yore is available at our fingertips.

Don't go looking for God in signs and wonders. He's not found in an image burnt into a potato chip or a sketchy manifestation of the Virgin Mary on the wall of a dank cavern somewhere. If you hear of signs and wonders, they are likely the work of a charlatan or could even be a snare prepared by Satan or his minions. Don't fall for the faith healers or ecstatic babblers who claim to be speaking in tongues with a message from God. Those things ceased with the last of the apostles. If you want to hear from God, open your Bible or go to a church where one of his shepherds faithfully preaches and teaches the full truth of the Scriptures. If you want to talk to God, pray to Him in accordance with His word and will in Jesus' name. If you don't know what to say, go to the Bible where Christ Himself instructs us how to pray.

Does God only work through the means of grace? Yes. He has chosen to work through word and sacrament. But that doesn't mean that He is not intimately involved in the lives of believers. He most certainly is. If we stay in His word and thusly fit ourselves with spiritual lenses we will see the evidence all around us. God and His holy angels are at work in ways that escape our attention. In heaven we will surely see how they have guided, directed and protected us in many miraculous ways unbeknownst to us in this life. Yet, miracles still abound that we can witness and experience every day. If we have trouble discerning them, we must remember to use God's good purposes as a gauge.

When we commune with the Lord at His table, His real body and blood are present in, with and under the earthly elements of wine and bread in a miraculous way. How do we know this? He tells us in His word (1 Corinthians 11:24-26). What is God's good purpose in this sacrament? It reminds us of what Christ did for us on the cross and provides us with the never-ending comfort and assurance of the forgiveness of our sins. It strengthens and helps to keep us in the faith unto life everlasting. When we see a baby baptized, we are most assuredly seeing a miracle. Through this sacrament, we have witnessed someone being brought to faith in Jesus by the power of the Holy Spirit working through God's word. This can only be accomplished by God and none other. It's the word and not the water. That earthly element was given to us by God to help us comprehend the miraculous, spiritual washing and regeneration of a sinful human being. We were all dead in our trespasses and sins and completely unable to apprehend faith by our own decision or power (Ephesians 2:1 and John 15:16). We were enemies of God from conception but were transformed and made new in spirit (Psalm 51:5 and 2 Corinthians 5:17). Now, that's what I call a miracle!

If we're new creations in Christ and we are in the word, Jesus constantly performs miracles in our lives. Others may not notice it, but we know. Has God ever quelled your anger and given you a heart filled with reconciliation? Has He calmed your fear and granted you true peace? Has the Lord empowered you to do His work and then blessed you with true joy in doing so? If you have any doubts, just pray to God in Jesus' name and ask Him for a chance to share the good news of salvation with someone. You might be surprised at how swiftly and assuredly He responds.

When we pray, we must remember two things. First, God may answer yes, no, or wait on Him and be patient. If we pray in accordance with His word and will in Jesus' name, He will definitely answer. If we give it time and trust in His perfect wisdom and will rather than our own feeble reason, He will most assuredly respond. We may not get what we think is best for us in a temporal sense but He will always do what is best for us ... in accordance with His good purposes which always accrue to our benefit, first and foremost, in terms of eternal salvation.

To best understand the blessings bestowed on so many people at Lutheran North, in the midst of the chaos that engulfed Ferguson, requires the light of God's providence.

Our lives are filled with many such true miracles. If we are to discern whether a miracle has occurred, we need to keep these things in mind:

- Has something occurred that seems to exceed the bounds of natural law?

- Has God intervened in a supernatural way?
- What good purpose of God has been served in accordance with His plan of salvation for sinful mankind?

As we take stock of our lives, may God's word in the Holy Bible serve as our guide and may we remember to keep our spiritual lenses firmly in place.

COVER PICTURES

Front Cover: Coach Simmons and the Lutheran North Crusaders at Lamothe Field after winning the 2014 District Championship.

Back Cover (Top Left Photo): Back Row Coaches Josh Cody, Troy Fehrs, Brian Simmons, Jon Mueller and Steve Stranghoener. Front Row Coaches Mike Williams, Kelvin Austin, Mike Lorenz and Steve Maneikis (Matt Hieke not pictured)

Back Cover (Top Right Photo): 2015 Crusaders at half-time of state quarterfinal game against Palmyra … down 28-0.

Back Cover (Bottom Left Photo): "Big C" Coach Carl Reed, Jr.

Other books by Steve Stranghoener:

Deadly Preference

Veeper

God-Whacked

Cha-Cha Chandler: Teen Demonologist

Straight Talk About Christian Misconceptions

Murder By Chance: Blood Moon Lunacy of
Lew Carew

Asunder: The Tale of the Renaissance Killer

The Last Prophet: Doomsday Diary

The Last Prophet: Imminent End

Tracts in Time

Available at Amazon.com

55749931R00179

Made in the USA
Charleston, SC
05 May 2016